Jim Hunter was Headmaster of a boys' school in Reading, England. He is now a lecturer at the Open University. His other work includes *Top Stoppard's Plays* (Faber, 1982) and he is the editor of two volumes of *Modern Short Stories* (Faber, 1993, 1994). He is also the author of several novels.

Bill Naismith, the series editor of the Faber Critical Guides, was a Lecturer in Drama and English at the University of London, Goldsmiths' College, for twenty-five years and now lectures in drama for the University of Iowa in London. His other published work includes student guides to *'Top Girls' by Caryl Churchill* (Methuen, 1991), *'The Rover' by Aphra Behn* (Methuen, 1993), *'Across Oka' by Robert Holman* (Methuen, 1994) and *'Our Country's Good' by Timberlake Wertenbaker* (Methuen, 1993).

FABER CRITICAL GUIDES
Series Editor: Bill Naismith

SAMUEL BECKETT
(*Waiting for Godot, Endgame, Krapp's Last Tape*)
by John Fletcher

BRIAN FRIEL
(*Philadelphia, Here I Come!, Translations, Making History,
Dancing at Lughnasa*)
by Nesta Jones

SEAN O'CASEY
(*The Shadow of a Gunman, The Plough and the Stars,
Juno and the Paycock*)
by Christopher Murray

HAROLD PINTER
(*The Birthday Party, The Caretaker, The Homecoming*)
by Bill Naismith

A FABER CRITICAL GUIDE
Tom Stoppard

Rosencrantz and Guildenstern Are Dead

Jumpers

Travesties

Arcadia

JIM HUNTER

faber and faber

LONDON·NEW YORK

Published . . . . ber Inc.,
an affiliate of Farrar, Straus and Giroux, New York

Photoset by Wilmaset Ltd, Birkenhead, Wirral
Printed in England by Mackays of Chatham plc, Chatham, Kent

Grateful acknowledgement is made to
Grove/Atlantic, Inc., for permission to use excerpts from
Jumpers, Rosencrantz and Guildenstern Are Dead and *Travesties*
by Tom Stoppard in the edition of this book published in the US.
Copyright © 1967, 1972, and 1975 by Tom Stoppard.
Reprinted by permission of Grove/Atlantic, Inc.

A CIP record for this book
is available from the British Library
ISBN 0-571-19782-5

2 4 6 8 10 9 7 5 3 1

Contents

CONTENTS

Editor's Preface

The *Faber Critical Guides* provide comprehensive intro-
ductions to major dramatists of the twentieth century.

The need to make an imaginative leap when reading
dramatic texts is well known. Plays are written with live
performance in mind. Often a theatre audience is confronted with a stage picture, a silent character or a vital
movement – any of which might be missed in a simple
'reading'. The *Guides* advise you what to look for.

All plays emerge from a context – a background – the
significance of which may vary but needs to be appreci-
ated if the original impact of the play is to be understood.
A writer may be challenging theatrical convention, react-
ing to the social and political life of the time or engaging
with intellectual ideas. The *Guides* provide coverage of
the appropriate context in each case.

A number of key texts are examined in each *Guide* in
order to provide a sound introduction to the individual
dramatists. Studying only one work is rarely enough to
make informed judgements about the style and originality
of writer's work. Considering several plays is also the
only way to follow a writer's development.

Finally, the *Guides* are meant to be read in conjunction
with the play texts. 'The play's the thing' and must always
be the primary concern. Not only are all playwrights
different but every play has its own distinctive features
which the *Guides* are concerned to highlight.

Note on References

There are few quotations in this book from critics, and each is identified as it occurs. There are many quotations from Tom Stoppard himself in interview, and references to these are abbreviated. A key interview is the long one given to the editors of *Theatre Quarterly*, issue 14, May–July 1974, quotations from which are identified by the name of the magazine. Other interviews were given in 1976 to Ronald Hayman and included in his very useful short study: *Contemporary Playwrights: Tom Stoppard* (Heinemann, 1979); quotations from these are identified by Hayman's name.

Other quotations come from *Conversations with Stoppard* by Mel Gusson, Nick Hern Books, 1995, and a large anthology, *Tom Stoppard In Conversation*, edited by Paul Delaney, University of Michigan Press, 1994 (which also reprinted the *Theatre Quarterly* interview). These are identified by the words *In Conversation* followed by the name of the particular interviewer.

Page references to the plays by Stoppard under discussion are to the single editions of the plays published by Faber (re-set in 2000). For each quotation from *Rosencrantz and Guildenstern Are Dead*, *Jumpers* and *Travesties*, two page references are given: the first is to the Faber edition, the second is to the edition published by Grove in the United States. In the chapter on *Jumpers*, where a single page reference is given, this is to the Faber edition, which incorporates changes to the text made for the 1984 production at the Aldwych Theatre in London and includes a Coda substantially different from that in the Grove edition (see pages 79–80 for a discussion of the different Codas).

References to *Rosencrantz and Guildenstern Are Dead*: when Shakespeare's play alone is intended, the attendant lords are given their full names; concerning Stoppard's play specifically, they are called Ros and Guil; when both plays are equally meant, they are noted simply R. and G.

I am grateful to Gay Firth and Alistair Randall for bringing material to my notice, and to Jerry Burridge for help with Stoppard's references to physics and mathematics.

J.H.

Introduction

Tom Stoppard spoke English from an early age and has lived in England since he was nine. His writing shows a delight in English language and literature, and at one point uses the particularly English example of a cricket bat as an emblem of craftsmanship. Yet he was actually born Czech, as Thomas Straussler, in 1937; and was twice an infant refugee: first from the Nazis in 1939 and then in 1942 from Singapore and the Japanese, at which time his father died – 'in enemy hands, and that's that' (quoted by Kenneth Tynan in *Show People*).

In Darjeeling, in northern India, his mother worked for the Czech shoe company Bata, who had employed his father, and Tom boarded at an American multi-racial school. In 1946 his mother married Major Kenneth Stoppard and the family moved to England. Tom went to boarding prep school ('a privileged education, a lovely house, acres of parkland, we had a lovely time': *Sunday Times*, 1974) and on to a senior independent school. The danger and crises of his early childhood were followed by a relatively fortunate upbringing, in peacetime and in a stable country. This sequence in Stoppard's life – repeated danger overlaid by apparent security – almost certainly contributed to his later personality and to the plays we shall be studying; and I return to it in the final chapter of this book (p. 235).

Stoppard left school in 1954, aged seventeen and 'thoroughly bored by the idea of anything intellectual

... alienated by everyone from Shakespeare to Dickens' (*Theatre Quarterly*). For nine years he worked as a journalist in Bristol, eventually trying his hand at fiction and plays. In 1963 he moved to London, his first TV play was shown and a novel was commissioned; this was followed by plays for BBC Radio (including five episodes of *The Dales*, a radio soap with a huge regular audience) and short stories in a hardback anthology. Stoppard's apprenticeship was similar to that of most eventually successful dramatists: hard graft, gaining professional expertise by reviewing and writing playscripts for whatever market could be found.

The breakthrough year was 1966, when *Rosencrantz and Guildenstern Are Dead* was acclaimed at the Edinburgh Festival. For well over thirty years since then, Stoppard has consistently held his position as one of England's most admired and enjoyed dramatists. He was knighted – becoming Sir Tom – in 1997. In addition to his own plays, he has scripted adaptations of European comedies and the screenplays of many films, including the 1999 success, *Shakespeare in Love*. He often attends rehearsals of his new plays, rarely making a direct intervention but remaining on hand to consider redrafting a line or a whole scene; and directors and actors consistently say his presence is helpful.

Stoppard has been married twice and has four grown-up sons. He prefers to keep a low public profile, but emerged in the 1970s and 1980s to be politically active in human-rights protests against Communist regimes in the Soviet Union and Eastern Europe. In 1977 he made his first return visit to Czechoslovakia, and became a friend of the dramatist Vaclav Havel, who at the time was just released from prison (he was re-imprisoned later) and eventually became the country's first president after Communist rule. Stoppard describes himself as conservative, and is half-way religious – 'I approve of belief in God and I try to behave as if there is one, but that hardly amounts to faith' (*In Conversation: Guppy*). What he does firmly defend is his belief in moral absolutes: 'The difference between moral rules and the rules of tennis is that the rules of tennis can be changed' (see *Jumpers*, p. 40/49).

Theatre, Stoppard says in the preface to a collection of his plays, is 'first and foremost a recreation', and his own writing (screenplays apart) intends to make us smile or laugh. He gives us groan-worthy puns as well as dazzling ones, and sometimes an overlap with broad popular farce. Yet, in the four plays studied here, serious questions are never that far away, and are never in themselves mocked. When Guil puzzles about death, or George about God, or when Joyce pontificates about art, we can smile at the human inadequacies of the characters, but we are not invited to smile at their concerns. These comic plays are set against backgrounds of basic enquiry into reality itself, and into how human beings should conduct themselves. The plays themselves don't claim to advance such enquiry; they remain *plays*, entertainments, inviting us to smile. And this has troubled some spectators, who perhaps feel vaguely that it's all right to laugh at, say, a fat man caught in a revolving door, but not a philosopher wrestling with the problem of Goodness. Stoppard, I suspect, sees the latter as potentially just as funny, and the dimensions of revolving doors as much less interesting than the problem of Goodness. That doesn't mean that his play even begins to *solve* the problem, any more than

3

an enjoyable sit-com can solve problems of family tensions.

In a Stoppard play we can expect to find three particular elements: *brilliant language*; *absurd yet inspired theatrical ideas*; and *an intellectual frame of reference* which is not mocked, whatever else is.

The *brilliant language* is never far away. Try the speeches of the Player in *Rosencrantz*, Dotty in *Jumpers*, or everyone in *Travesties*. Or Septimus Hodge, on page 9 of *Arcadia*, running verbal rings round Ezra Chater who thinks that *he* is the poet. There are puns at the level of stand-up comedy (Bones–Foot–Jumper, *Jumpers*, p. 55/ 58), one-liners ('If I'm going to arrest her, I can hardly do it by Interflora,' *Jumpers*, p. 34/45), and innumerable verbal contests (much of *Rosencrantz*, for example). And there are long virtuoso speeches, toppling towers of language, most spectacular in *Travesties* but found even in the relative realism of *Arcadia* (try Thomasina and Septimus, p. 50).

Stoppard's most famous *theatrical idea* is one of his first: to set a play 'within and around the action of *Hamlet*', and make two attendant lords the main characters, so that we see them holding a rueful post-mortem on a brief fragment of Shakespeare's play ('He murdered us ... Twenty-seven-three.' *Rosencrantz*, p. 48/ 57). A similar notion led to *The Real Inspector Hound*, in which the lives of critics watching a stale thriller are farcically confused with the action onstage. A more complex development is the modelling of *Travesties* on the template of Oscar Wilde's *The Importance of Being Earnest* – the very play over which two of the characters squabbled in real life. *Hamlet* turns up again in *Dogg's Hamlet*, which brings together Shakespeare, a school speech day, and a linguistic 'investigation' by the philosopher Ludwig Wittgenstein; the second half of the evening is *Cahoot's Macbeth*, based on the fact that leading Czech actors, banned for political reasons, were putting on shortened performances in private flats: here *Macbeth* is raided by an inspector of police, whose appearances coincide with those of Shakespeare's disputed Third Murderer and Banquo's Ghost.

This doesn't mean that all Stoppard's theatrical ideas use other people's plays. *Jumpers*, which is about philosophy, opens with an acrobatic display and has the plot of a murder story. *Every Good Boy Deserves Favour* requires a symphony orchestra on stage. *Night and Day* seems essentially realistic, yet we are allowed to hear the inner thoughts of one character and for a while even see her fantasy self in a fantasy encounter; and *The Real Thing* opens with a gripping scene which we later discover to be from a stage play being written by a third character. In the 1990s, Stoppard has written three plays where different historical periods alternate and overlap on stage. Though one of his best plays was a realist drama for television (*Professional Foul*, 1977), theatre for Stoppard means theatricality, showbiz, a faint whiff of a conjuring act or a circus.

As for the *intellectual frame of reference* in so many of his plays, it may seem surprising from the man who quit school 'totally bored' at seventeen. But he turns out to write about people involved in philosophy, advanced mathematics and physics, and Latin and Greek scholarship. His speciality is to flick this intellectual material into the air so spectacularly that it becomes entertaining.

The plays studied in this book make me think of a bunch of street-dancers or skaters, raiding some great historic buildings – a cathedral, say, a palace, and a place of government. They perform clattering jumps up and down the wide stairways, and swerve brilliantly round massive pillars; their noise and cries echo in vast spaces. Watching and enjoying this disrespectful yet skilful display, we still don't lose sight of the huge buildings themselves, or of what they stand for. Stoppard's plays present a unique interplay between fun and the most basic and serious challenges to human understanding. He writes jokes and comic routines; but at the same time he is also writing about moral responsibility, about goodness, and about our scientific, mathematical or philosophical understanding of reality.

Some of the point of the dancers' display is lost if we have no previous knowledge of the great buildings they are raiding. This is particularly true for *Rosencrantz*, which assumes a knowledge of Shakespeare's *Hamlet* and Beckett's *Waiting for Godot*; and for *Travesties*, which takes it for granted that we know *The Importance of Being Earnest*. These are the essential master-works which form the structural bases for Stoppard's parodies. *Jumpers* and *Arcadia* do not lean on previous theatre in such a way, and to that extent can be taken more on their own terms, though I hope my notes will show how much they too are dancing within cathedrals.

Context and Background

Born fifteen years earlier, Tom Stoppard might never have become a playwright at all. Nor for that matter might William Shakespeare, if born in 1549 rather than 1564. The man and the time need to coincide.

In 1954, when Stoppard left school, English theatre was about to be transformed. The next five years brought to London Samuel Beckett's *Waiting for Godot*, John Osborne's *Look Back in Anger*, Bertolt Brecht's Berliner Ensemble, Joan Littlewood's Theatre Workshop, and plays by Harold Pinter, Arnold Wesker and John Arden. Collectively these had relatively little in common, but each looked like a liberator when compared with the standard English drama of the time, gridlocked in middle-class talk in country houses. In Stoppard's own words to *Theatre Quarterly*: 'After 1956 everybody of my age who wanted to write, wanted to write plays.'

Beyond Realism

At that time, plays could seem fresh simply by being about ordinary people. More significant for Stoppard was the reaction against realism. For more than a century realist conventions had dominated Western theatre. Audiences were confronted by curtains closing off the stage under a proscenium arch; the opening of those curtains seemed to remove the fourth wall of a room, apparently fully furnished, where characters showed no awareness of being watched. Dialogue, too, had to seem realistic, which made it harder to get across basic information (who is who and where are we?) and led to mechanisms such as the one gleefully parodied in Stoppard's *The Real Inspector Hound*: the telephone informatively answered. Mrs Drudge the cleaning woman just happens to be dusting the phone; the moment it rings she '*snatches it up*' and announces: 'Hello, the drawing-room of Lady Muldoon's country residence one morning in early spring?'

Some reaction against this realist stranglehold had begun as early as the 1920s, among poets and other experimental dramatists. But mainstream theatre re-mained unaltered, and several young 1950s playwrights continued to accept realist conventions, feeling less bothered about changing theatre than about changing society. And realism remains alive and well today: it makes up almost all the drama we normally watch (e.g. in Britain, *EastEnders*) because it's the natural mode of the camera. Film and television present much more accurate detail and yet can cut ruthlessly from significant moment to moment, far faster than stage realism. Theatre, we might say, has handed realism on, to the screen, and now with relief returns to what it does best, which is gathering a live audience together to see a *representation* which need not be a full *simulation*. Furniture, moods or vast spaces can be indicated by a gesture or two; within a few minutes the same actors can play quite different characters in completely altered settings; information can be given direct to the audience; action may slide into dance, and song or poetry or lavishly heightened speech may replace plodding prosaic dialogue.

Without this liberation, and the excitement surrounding it, Stoppard might never have started writing plays.

Plays Inside Plays

Hamlet, the most famous play of the supreme dramatist, and the setting for Stoppard's first success, is itself partly about acting – seen not as something done just by professionals, but by all of us at times. Acting interests us, and yet because it falsifies reality it is dangerous. Early on, Hamlet himself decides to act mad, partly in order to deceive his family and partly in order to postpone having to take actual 'action' himself. He's unsure whether to trust his father's ghost, who has ordered Hamlet to revenge his murder; the ghost could possibly have been a devil with the power to 'assume a pleasing shape'. On the arrival of a troupe of professional actors, Hamlet gets them to assume shapes too, in an instant display of their skill; and is fascinated yet appalled that the First Player can weep and turn pale with simulated grief. (The theatre audience observes skill at two levels: that of the real actor, and that of the actor he's acting.)

Hamlet arranges for a play, 'The Murder of Gonzago', resembling the murder of his father, to be watched by the murderer Claudius, who has been *acting* innocent and whose reactions Hamlet and his friend Horatio will be closely watching. The theatre audience then finds itself watching actors acting people watching more actors acting more people watching *still more* actors acting *yet more* actors acting *even more people* (Claudius and his Queen) who are themselves watching – and all of this is simultaneous, a multiple theatrical excitement. This example is particularly relevant for Stoppard; but there are innumerable other occasions in drama where stage characters themselves take part in play-acting. At the simplest level, actors dress up to play characters who then, in innumerable classical plays, put on a further layer of disguise. In twentieth-century theatre, stage characters often set up momentary 'plays' representing other scenes without even changing costume, in a casual role-play like that of young children.

Theatre, in other words, enjoys being highly self-conscious – fascinated by its own falseness, yet reckoning to reveal a kind of truth. At a serious level, it explores the whole relationship of illusion with reality; and at a comic level, it 'camps it up' – the phrase is associated with homosexuality, but it describes a deliberately overplayed style which anyone in the theatre can enjoy, and which indeed underlies Stoppard's *Travesties*. A play within a play capitalises on our enjoyment of play-acting, yet encourages us to be critical of what we see.

Modernism and the Theatre of the Absurd

Luigi Pirandello's *Six Characters in Search of an Author* (1921) gives a sharp new twist to this idea. Into a conventional theatre at rehearsal time (with bored actors and director standing around) walk six 'Characters', each wearing a face-mask defining their identity. They carry within them a powerful story, but their play itself has not yet been written. They persuade the actors to represent them on stage, but are then disappointed with the result: the actors perform too 'stagily', blinkered by past convention. The Characters find themselves insisting that they are more real than the actors who try to imitate them, because their 'reality' in art doesn't change. This 'immutable reality' is, however, 'terrible ... It should make you shudder to come near us.'

Pirandello was just one figure in the disruptive shift in Western culture which is called Modernism. Modernist art tended to be 'difficult' and challenged conventional expectations, and perhaps for those reasons took time to filter down the educational system. In my own school-days, which happened to be close to Tom Stoppard's both in years and geography, the early poetry of T. S. Eliot still seemed excitingly 'modern', and it became among Stoppard's favourites; so too did painters such as René Magritte, and the novelist Ernest Hemingway, about whom he once intended to write a play. *Travesties* of course features caricatures of two pioneer Modernists, James Joyce and Tristan Tzara. It seems that to under-stand influences on a writer who came to prominence in the 1960s, we might do best to look at the 1920s.

Negatively, Modernism was determined to reject nine-teenth-century practices which had become so highly developed that they seemed to have nowhere further to go – the all-knowing psychological novel, huge and lavish symphonies and operas, painting which simulated con-ventional or photographic perception. As with other artistic revolutions, it was sometimes linked with social or political anger: Tzara's Dadaists (Modernists of an extreme kind) felt that the Western society which was continuing to fund the First World War must be rotten to its very soul: i.e. its art. The task of a Dadaist must be to mock and 'smash' traditional art (*Travesties*, p. 53/41). Philosophically, Modernism often seemed grim, particu-larly in literature, where religious faith was shown in collapse and psychology was causing the individual to mistrust his free will, his subconscious motives and his very identity as a person, let alone his ability to communicate or love.

More positively, Modernism offered new ways of rendering reality: Cubist painting, collage (paralleled in the 'cut-up' technique of Eliot's *The Waste Land*), stream-of-consciousness writing such as that of Joyce or Virginia Woolf, and, in music, extensions of listeners' harmonic and rhythmic expectation. Being strange, 'difficult', 'intellectual' was almost a plus in itself: people needed to be shaken out of complacency, and the subtle crafting of a work of art was a high aim in life (see, of course, Joyce in *Travesties*). And though rebelling against its immediate predecessors, Modernism tended to be intensely interested in much older artistic traditions, both in early cultures (myth, ritual, dance) and Western master-pieces; Modernist art was full of allusions, some of which become parodies or indeed 'travesties'.

Much of this sounds like early Stoppard: disruptive effects, intellectual difficulty, individuals wondering who they are or what their purpose is, theatre and language constantly echoing and parodying themselves, street-dancing in cathedrals. By the 1960s, certain tricks of Modernism had become part of popular culture: a watered-down Cubism was common in newspaper cartoons, Stravinsky was echoed in the soundtracks of movie thrillers, and Dada lived again in the guitar-smashing rock bands.

A branch of Modernist theatre, emerging perhaps partly from Tzara's Dadaism, became known as the Theatre of the Absurd. This was at its height in the 1930s and 1940s, mostly in Paris; and it produced one great dramatist, the Irish-born Samuel Beckett, by then living in France. Absurdist theatre, as well as being Modernist-grotesque (rhinoceroses and elephants in suburbia), also tended to be cyclical (as was implied by the original ending of Stoppard's *Rosencrantz*). Life was seen to be going nowhere, and all conventional aims and purposes were considered pointless, absurd. Absurdist plays were typically both ludicrous and pessimistic; one leader in the field, Eugène Ionesco, commented that he wanted always to remind the spectator that he would become a corpse.

Rosencrantz in 1966 looked like the first work of a would-be Absurdist; arguably it derives more from Beckett's *Waiting for Godot* than from its setting in *Hamlet*. But it is altogether more exuberant, and gentler in tone, than most offerings from the Theatre of the Absurd; and ultimately simply less *serious*, much more concerned to provide a good evening out. This indeed led to some attacks from early critics who were determined to take it solemnly and then felt disappointed.

The true independent voice of Stoppard's theatre may come decked in Modernist clothes, yet has quite different inclinations. In his brilliant one-act play *After Magritte*, the lights go up on an utterly ludicrous scene: a domestic living room with various bodies in grotesque situations (for example, a man bare to the waist is standing on a chair wearing black evening-dress trousers and thigh-length green rubber waders). This looks obviously Modern and Absurd. But no: during the first half of the play everything in this opening tableau is gradually restored to normal, and rationally explained. At the moment of entire normality, a police inspector bursts in with the line, 'What is the meaning of this bizarre spectacle?' In the remainder of the play, again for entirely explicable reasons, a different but equally ludicrous tableau is again assembled; but this time we know at each point why. Nothing is 'bizarre' when it's explained; the world is saner than it looks. Something similar happens in Stoppard's radio play *Artist Descending a Staircase* (its title another reference to Modernist art): extremely suspicious circumstances turn out in the end to have an entirely innocent explanation.

The central character of Stoppard's only novel, *Lord Malquist and Mr Moon*, keeps finding that 'the commonplace had duped him into seeing absurdity' – though admittedly the sentence does continue, 'just as absurdity kept tricking him into accepting it as commonplace'. The mind behind these light-hearted plots is temperamentally disinclined to break up in Modernist despair, and is the same mind which twenty or more years later became fascinated by quantum physics. If the world looks chaotic, don't give up on it: try another angle of vision.

Stoppard takes particular delight in making the most unpromising material *fit* – which is why the conductor André Previn invited (challenged?) him to write a play which would require a symphony orchestra on stage; and why, in *Every Good Boy Deserves Favour*, he managed it. In *Cahoot's Macbeth*, the classic useless line of ancient phrase-books – 'His postilion has been struck by lightning' – actually turns out to be useful. Stoppard has spoken of the sheer joy, as he crafted *The Real Inspector Hound*, of finally realising – as if it was there already, unknown to him – that the body on stage is that of the missing critic Higgs. And having discovered, while writing *Travesties*, two perfect fits which were not of his own making (see this book, p. 114–15), Stoppard later described them to Ronald Hayman as 'almost like little signs from God that you're on the right track'.

It is of course a traditional craft of comedy, having

strewn the toys over the carpet, to then put them tidily away; in that, Stoppard was doing nothing new. But when in *Hapgood* and *Arcadia* he moves on to serious matters of the universe, to the apparent randomness of modern physics, it is with delighted interest rather than Modernist trepidation. The late twentieth-century 'chaos theory' which underpins *Arcadia* doesn't describe actual chaos – mere confusion and disorder – but *unpredictability*: definable mathematical processes can be observed, but we cannot know the pattern which will result. For the Stoppard who 'approves of belief in God' this may not be bad news, since it offers an exhilarating escape from Newtonian physics where, theoretically, if scientists were skilled enough, all the future could be known.

Post-modernism?

Post-modernism is a word of our times which by its very nature is hard to define. It generally refers to a kind of free-floating in intellectual space, having cast ourselves off from all past explanations of why things seem as they are – not only the explanation by Newtonian physics, but also those of religion, Marxism, psychoanalysis, even history. Each of these large-scale theories is considered no longer roadworthy – partly because of a mistrust of language itself. They are seen as fabrications, 'grand narratives' rather than truth. So if all that's available is one sort of fabrication or another, perhaps we might just as well have fun with the entirely artificial, a 'virtual reality'; with pastiche (imitation), parody, travesty.

This sounds pretty much a make-over of Sir Archibald Jumper's gymnastics. It may also seem relevant to *Travesties*, where various grand narratives are mocked, historical truth is constantly fractured, and a brilliant dance nevertheless goes on. As for language, although it is typically dazzling in these plays, it also poignantly falters, as in the meanderings of George and Carr in *Jumpers* and *Travesties* respectively. *Jumpers* dates from 1972, *Travesties* from 1974; so when in the 1980s smart people began to talk of post-modernism, Stoppard might reasonably have murmured that he'd already been there, showing his plays as his T-shirt.

But he might have added that 'there' wasn't somewhere he personally would wish to live. In *Jumpers* 'I wanted to suggest that atheists may be the cripples, lacking the strength to live with the idea of God' (*In Conversation: Kerensky.*) And on post-modernist free-floating he might well quote his philosopher Anderson, in *Professional Foul*:

> you can persuade a man to believe almost anything provided he is clever enough, but it is much more difficult to persuade someone less clever. There is a sense of right and wrong which precedes utterance.

The plays studied in this book struck their first audiences as attractively flashy, up with the times, perhaps trend-setting. But – at least from *Jumpers* onwards – they are sympathetic to traditional beliefs: the notions of absolute good (with a possible absolute judge), of natural innocence, and of the almost heroic importance of art. Stoppard's conservatism has always distanced him politically from most other dramatists of his day; and his seriousness about moral issues, coupled with an underlying trust in life, works as a kind of Trojan horse within the walls of Modernist doubt and post-modernist anarchy. A, more than minus A.

A and minus A

'Tom Stoppard Doesn't Know' was the title of a verbal and visual statement the playwright made for BBC Television in 1972. Later to Ronald Hayman he identified in himself the pattern 'firstly, A; secondly minus A'; or

> that particular cube which on one side says for example: 'All Italians are voluble' and on the next side says, 'That is a naïve generalisation'; and then, 'No. it's not. Behind generalisations there must be some sort of basis.'

Time and again Stoppard would come out with similar binary oppositions, and traced them in his writing.

> There is very often *no* single, clear statement in my plays. What there is, is a series of conflicting statements made by conflicting characters, and they tend to play out a sort of infinite leapfrog. (*Theatre Quarterly*)

This 'not knowing' clearly laid itself open to charges of fence-sitting; but seems rather to have represented a scrupulous integrity. It is important to tell the truth; essential not to pretend to certainties you don't actually have. The 'infinite leapfrog' in plays can lead to structural problems which will be touched on later. In human terms the 'A, minus A' opposition was effectively dramatised in Stoppard's novel *Lord Malquist and Mr Moon*. Lord Malquist is a dandy, Moon an innocent who wants to find goodness.

The Dandy and the Would-be-good

'Dandy' is not a word much used today. It is, however, the way Stoppard describes Sir Archibald Jumper; and also, in 1986 (*In Conversation*, p. 5), how he felt himself to be seen by others, as 'this dandified wit'; he then added, in a typical 'A, minus A' formulation: 'It's all true and false.' The original meaning of the word was a fop, someone ostentatiously well-dressed, and it tended to extend to smart ways of behaving and talking. A dandy looked elegant, was socially sophisticated, and knew it. On the other hand he showed no interest in matters of conscience or morality.

The young Stoppard was elegant, a sharp dresser and good-looking, with some resemblance to his friend (and dandy of a sort) Mick Jagger. He was also a brilliant talker, yet fastidious about finding the right word and even in articulating it. He admired the deft style of Evelyn Waugh and – the most famous dandy in English letters – Oscar Wilde, who hovers ambivalently behind much of his work and actually appears on stage in *The Invention of Love* (1997). Lord Malquist, in Stoppard's novel, tends to echo Wilde: 'substance is ephemeral but style is eternal' (a Wilde character says: 'In matters of grave importance, style, not sincerity, is the thing'). And Malquist is utterly callous to the most obvious suffering.

Moon, in contrast, is 'wide-open' to everything from the starving in Asia to the wiping-out of the white rhino. And, oddly, Stoppard also gave the same name to other early innocents. 'Moon,' he said, 'is a person to whom things happen.' Then he added: 'I'm a Moon myself.' Certainly, Moon in the novel sounds very like the young Stoppard when he says:

> I cannot commit myself to either side of a question. Because if you attach yourself to one or the other you disappear into it. And I can't even side with the balance

of morality because I don't know whether morality is an instinct or just an imposition.

This may be fence-sitting, but it is the opposite extreme from dandyism: here is a character so morally anxious that he questions the impulse to morality itself. The relevance to the struggle of ideas between George and Archie will be clear to students of *Jumpers*. There the dramatist's own sympathies are unquestionably with George, but the flashy, glittering manner of the play itself (and later of *Travesties*) might appear to side more with theatrical dandyism. Stoppard's work can easily be underestimated by those who assume that it offers dandyism and not much else.

Rosencrantz and Guildenstern Are Dead

In Shakespeare's *Hamlet*, Rosencrantz and Guildenstern are two relatively minor courtiers. But in Stoppard's play they are the central characters, always on stage. The rough idea had been used nearly a century earlier by W. S. Gilbert (later of 'Gilbert and Sullivan'), but whereas his verse-nonsense altered the course of Shakespeare's play, here *Hamlet* remains inviolable, a predetermined scheme which finally drowns the stage in 'dark and music'. Fragments of Shakespeare are seen, but most of the action of *Rosencrantz* seems to happen just outside *Hamlet*'s borders. So, for example, on p. 47/56 Hamlet and Polonius leave the stage to continue the action in Shakespeare, and Ros and Guil are left behind.

Ros and Guil can just about remember being called to court this morning, but nothing previously. They know what they are here for – to find out what is troubling Hamlet – but they cannot see a future for themselves after that. They seem to be confined to the stage, and ordinary chance – where coins fall different ways up at different times – seems to have deserted them. For them everything seems predestined.

Though they are dressed as Elizabethans, Stoppard gives them twentieth-century intellects. They attempt to make sense of their situation by rational means – we get scraps of traditional philosophical enquiry – yet they mistrust all perceptions. They are also modern in their fear of death as extinction, and the action of *Hamlet* never allows them to forget death for long. Yet although *Rosencrantz* is set on the fringes of a famous tragedy, and touches on profound questions, its prime aim is entertainment, and particularly comedy. It smiles ruefully at our perplexities, rather than offering a serious investigation of them.

It also smiles at the nature of theatre itself, in this much helped by the intermittent presence of travelling players based loosely on those who appear in *Hamlet*.

Two Background Texts

Art is sometimes said to draw on previous art as much as on real life. In Stoppard's case this is certainly so. Two of the world's best-known plays, *Hamlet* and *Waiting for Godot*, lie obviously behind *Rosencrantz*.

Hamlet
The following summary deals only with what is directly relevant to Stoppard's play:

The Danish King, Hamlet's father, has recently died, and his brother Claudius has taken the throne and married his queen, Gertrude. The former King's ghost tells Hamlet he was poisoned by Claudius, and demands revenge. But Hamlet hesitates, concealing his knowledge under an 'antic disposition' – a pretence of madness. Claudius summons to court Rosencrantz and Guildenstern, who grew up with Hamlet, to engage him in conversation and find out what's on his mind. But Hamlet proves far too clever for them (see *Rosencrantz*, pp. 46–7/56–7).

A group of travelling players arrives at court. Hamlet

21

sets up a play, 'The Murder of Gonzago', which closely resembles the murder of his father. At the performance Claudius is guiltily shocked, but Hamlet fails to take the opportunity to accuse him in public (and, a little later, to kill him in private). Instead, he kills an eavesdropper in the Queen's room who turns out to be Polonius, Denmark's devious chief minister. Claudius sends Hamlet on a voyage to England, along with Rosencrantz and Guildenstern, who carry a sealed letter ordering that on arrival there he is to be killed. Hamlet intercepts the letter, rewrites it to order the execution of Rosencrantz and Guildenstern instead, and escapes from the ship during a highly convenient pirate attack. The title of Stoppard's play is quoted from the last pages of Shakespeare's.

Hamlet depicts a corrupt, treacherous court in which people deviously use others for their own advantage; and the two most obviously used are Rosencrantz and Guildenstern. T. S. Eliot's poem 'The Love-Song of J. Alfred Prufrock' seems to have them in mind:

> No! I am not Prince Hamlet, nor was meant to be;
> Am an attendant lord, one that will do
> To swell a progress, start a scene or two,
> Advise the prince; no doubt, an easy tool...

– a tool, that is, not only for those at court but also, as it were, for a supernatural Dramatist. This looks like Stoppard's starting-point; significantly he quotes Eliot's poem several times in *Lord Malquist and Mr Moon*, published in the same week as the first performance of *Rosencrantz*. (The novel also includes a character writing 'a monograph on *Hamlet* as a source of book titles'.)

Rosencrantz puts two attendant lords centre stage, unlike heroes they are deprived of freedom of action; know they are being used, but not for what purpose or by what God or Dramatist – if any.

Hamlet himself, in Shakespeare, is a brooding intellectual, questioning everything: already what in the 1950s was called an anti-hero. Stoppard effectively transfers such doubts to Ros and Guil: in this modern view, attendant lords have minds and feelings too. Additionally, they are far more likely than a tragic hero to experience problems of identity. Shakespeare doesn't even allow Rosencrantz and Guildenstern separate personalities. Because they are falsely polite whenever they appear, they seem faceless and interchangeable: early on, as if to make this point, their names are switched in otherwise identical verse-lines (this is wittily choreographed in *Rosencrantz* on p. 28/36-7). Stoppard plays repeatedly on this: everyone muddles up Ros and Guil – even they themselves do so. Yet in his play they are given different temperaments; and whereas Rosencrantz and Guildenstern are spies who attract little or no sympathy, Ros and Guil are likeable, and 'a couple of bewildered innocents' (*In Conversation: Giles Gordon*).

In Shakespeare, Hamlet buys time by acting, pretending to be mad. This allows him to score points freely off everyone (in Stoppard, p. 48/57: 'He murdered us'), and it excites him almost to hysteria. Yet even as he is fascinated by it, he is appalled by other people's ability to put on a false face: a professional actor's skill is 'monstrous' (in Shakespeare this means offending against Nature itself); the King himself 'can smile, and smile, and be a villain'; and women's very beauty may make the whole sex corrupt. No appearance can be trusted any longer; the one final certainty, which even face-paint 'an inch thick' cannot deny, is the skull beneath the skin: eventual death. Much of this, though at a lighter level, spills over into Stoppard's play, including its climax (pp. 114–16/123–4) about acting death.

Waiting for Godot

Samuel Beckett was Irish by birth, but from his mid-twenties lived in France, and most of his work first appeared in French. His best-known play, *Waiting for Godot* – first performed in Paris in 1953 – develops primarily French ideas of the Theatre of the Absurd.

Vladimir and Estragon are two tramp-like clowns who meet on a country road in the evening to wait for Mr Godot to arrive. Instead of coming, Godot sends his apologies, via a boy-servant. Two other characters pass by and provide distraction. In the second act, the same pattern is followed, with variations: one early description of the play was that 'nothing happens, twice'. We get the strong sense that Vladimir and Estragon may turn up every evening for ever, yet that Godot will never come.

Beckett's play is both desperate and very funny. At the most basic level it shows how two characters doing nothing, and complaining of boredom, can occupy stage-time, exasperating and yet amusing their audience; it was soon imitated by scriptwriters for British radio and television (*Hancock's Half-Hour, Steptoe and Son*), and it prepared the way for the semi-realist plays of Harold Pinter. Some of the play is slapstick comedy – the moment on Stoppard's p. 82/89 when Ros removes his belt and his trousers slide down derives from Beckett, who of course got it from circus or pantomime. Its basic mode is two-man cross-talk, as in, say, Morecambe and Wise and as intimated in much of *Rosencrantz* (e.g., pp. 33–43/41–50).

Yet Beckett calls his play 'a tragicomedy'. And as well as laughter, he builds in many melancholy pauses: one critic wrote that 'silence is pouring into this play like water into a sinking ship'. Audiences seem expected to share, up to a point, the boredom and frustration of the characters on stage; and are likely to feel that the play must therefore be symbolic, and ultimately serious. The cross-talk is interrupted by portentous references to Christianity (in the old days, 'they crucified quick') or the human condition ('They give birth astride of a grave'); and the suggestion of the English 'God' in the French name Godot is teasingly confirmed when we are told that Mr Godot keeps his sheep and goats separately.

Waiting for Godot is the most popular of Beckett's works, but his many other writings show the same highly distinctive combination of structural elegance, farcical humour and the darkest pathos. His subject-matter is the frustration of all human yearning – for a meaning to life (or to plays), for health and happiness, for love. His characters are not only physically frustrated – by illness, senility, physical handicap, burial up to the neck or in a dustbin – but also mentally blocked: fragments of philosophical enquiry get side-tracked, or repeatedly recycled, or interrupted. And yet they keep trying again, just as Beckett himself spoke of artists having 'nothing to express, nothing with which to express, nothing from which to express, no power to express, no desire to express,' and *yet* 'the obligation to express'.

To some extent Ros and Guil are sufferers from the Beckett condition, dropped into the action of *Hamlet*. They are marginally more coherent than Beckett's characters in their struggle to make sense of their situation; but in the end they are equally defeated:

> GUIL: ... there must have been a moment, at the beginning, when we could have said – no. But somehow we missed it.

Rosencrantz: A Synopsis

In Act One Ros and Guil, two well-dressed Elizabethans, are betting on the toss of a coin. Ros, who is backing 'heads', always wins. They begin to fear (p. 7/17) they are 'within un-, sub- or supernatural forces'. They recall (p. 10/19) being summoned to court, at dawn; but have no idea why.

The Tragedians enter (p. 12/21). They are very down-at-heel actors, reduced to bloody sensationalism and a feeble pornography dependent on the boy-player, Alfred, pulling on his skirt. When they leave (p. 25/34), two scenes from *Hamlet* follow – Hamlet silently intruding on Ophelia (offstage in Shakespeare), and Claudius instructing Rosencrantz and Guildenstern to spy on Hamlet. Afterwards Ros and Guil are bewildered; but 'follow instructions ... Till events have played themselves out.' They try, unpromisingly, to rehearse their coming interrogation of Hamlet (p. 38ff/46ff), and the act ends as, in Shakespeare's lines, they greet him.

Act Two starts, again in Shakespeare, as Hamlet leaves them. Not only has he revealed little, he has confused Ros and Guil further (p. 46/56). Now they wait for someone else to come, something else to happen. A scrap of Shakespeare, setting up the play in which Hamlet hopes to trap Claudius (p. 53/62), leaves the chief Player on stage.

When Ros and Guil complain of not knowing what to do next, the Player advises them to 'Relax. Respond. That's what people do.' They share theories about what is wrong with Hamlet. After the Player leaves (p. 61/69), Ros calls 'Next!' but no one else comes. Ros broods on death (and the audience uneasily remember the play's title).

In a further scrap of Shakespeare (p. 64/72), Ros and Guil lyingly assure the King and Queen that their meeting with Hamlet went well. Next Hamlet is seen alone, contemplating suicide, after which he goes off with Ophelia. A figure dressed as the Queen enters and Ros, by now desperate to interrupt *somebody* in the know, puts his hands over her eyes and says 'Guess who?' It turns out to be the boy-player, Alfred; and we watch a rehearsal of 'The Murder of Gonzago'. But whereas that play was a re-enactment of events past, this one develops beyond Shakespeare into an anticipation of things *ahead* – the voyage, and the sealed orders – including two actors dressed just like Ros and Guil, who on arrival in England are promptly killed ... (p. 77/84). An uneasy discussion ensues, about whether real death is more convincing than an actor's rendering of it. Claudius is heard offstage interrupting the play; then appears to send Ros and Guil to seek Hamlet.

But (pp. 8off/89ff) they seem tied to the stage. Hamlet must come to them, which he duly does, with Polonius's body. After more fragments of Shakespeare, Ros and Guil hope that their work is done, but leave muttering that 'anything could happen yet'.

Act Three begins in darkness (p. 88/97). After a caricature of nautical sound-effects, Ros and Guil grasp that they are 'on a boat', and that Hamlet is sleeping nearby. They have an immediate purpose – to deliver 'the letter' to the English king – but (p. 96/105) cannot visualise their function or existence beyond that. More discussion of death. Ros wants to thwart whoever is controlling them. They open the letter, discover that it requires Hamlet's death, and suffer a very brief crisis of conscience – but then decide to seal up the letter again.

'*Impossibly*' (stage-direction, p. 105/114) the Tragedians climb out of barrels, as stowaways. Ros and Guil review the story so far, and Ros complains there isn't enough 'action'; instantly the pirates attack – another stage caricature. When the noise dies down, Hamlet has gone. Ros and Guil panic, re-open the letter, and now find their own names down for execution (p. 113/122). The Player is unmoved: 'In our experience, most things end in death'. This provokes an outburst from Guil, who sinks the Player's dagger deep into him. The ensuing death is impressive: the Tragedians applaud, after which the Player stands up, gratified. All the Tragedians then demonstrate their skills in dying, as darkness falls on them.

Ros and Guil are more baffled than ever. Ros disappears. Guil calls to him – trying both their names – then also disappears. The play fades out within Shakespeare's words.

'All the world's a stage'

... and all the men and women merely players.

Shakespeare's *As You Like It*, from which these words come, possibly opened the Globe Theatre in 1599, under the same motto in its Latin form: *totus mundus agit histrionem*. The comparison was already ancient; and we have many modern equivalents, talking of people who are 'acting out' or 'acting up', 'playing a role' or 'going through the motions'. From a religious point of view the idea might be reassuring: we are playing a part in a story understood and controlled by God, though not by us. The less comforting – and much commoner – view is that just as theatre is essentially an illusion, however persuasive, our 'real' lives may amount to little more. The comparison of life to play-acting occurs many times in Shakespeare, and in his last play, *The Tempest*, at the end of a play-within-a-play, we are told that 'the great globe itself ... shall dissolve ... like this insubstantial pageant faded.'

Shakespeare himself, however, had already used in some of his sonnets the opposite and equally traditional notion: *in a poem, beauty can last*. Reality may be questionable, worldly life may fade and die; but a work of art stands beyond mortality, fixed as itself. John Keats brooded on the 'truth' in the pictures on the side of an urn from ancient Greece; W. B. Yeats dreamed of becoming an artefact, a golden bird hammered out by the gold-smiths of Byzantium.

Golden birds are all very well, but if you discover you're a character locked forever inside the fixity of art, that's a nightmare. This is where many early spectators assumed that *Rosencrantz* was indebted to Luigi Pirandello's *Six Characters in Search of an Author* (see above, p. 10). Stoppard had in fact no direct knowledge of Pirandello, but may have absorbed him at second hand from *Next Time I'll Sing to You* by his friend James Saunders (who is credited with suggesting to Stoppard the expansion into a full-length play of his original verse-sketch about R. and G.). The terror of fixity felt by Pirandello's Characters is shared at the start of *Rosencrantz* by Guil, as the coins keep falling heads up. To a mathematician this might seem 'a spectacular vindication ...' etc. (p. 6/16), but to common sense it is a denial of the 'reassuring' element of chance (p. 8) 'which we recognised as nature'. The difference is that Pirandello's Characters know their story, whereas Ros and Guil know only their first instructions. The Characters hope for liberation by having their story performed; but when Ros and Guil's story is performed in dumbshow in front of them (pp. 74–5/80), they feel more grimly trapped than before: since the play is fixed and 'written', they are in a sense already (as in the title line) 'dead'.

What the situation does offer at a lower level, as in Beckett's play, is the opportunity for many in-jokes about theatre itself. These start almost immediately (p. 2/12) when, after five 'Heads' from Ros, Guil is allowed to say: 'There is an art to the building of suspense.' Cue for laugh of (provisional) relief from already uneasy audience. Similar jokes follow. This, like *Godot*, is a play intensely conscious of its own theatricality, and therefore inevitably ironic.

The illusion created by actors interests us, pleases us, may gratify our fantasies; many spectators identify with Hamlet and gleefully score the points with him. And when theatre seems to create a virtual reality, it tempts not just our emotions but our intellect; like a mind-altering drug, it may seem to offer new insights – and to unstable personalities may be equally dangerous. By their very nature, plays tend to deal in issues of illusion and reality; and they may offer parallels to our world.

This seems to be why Stoppard brings the Tragedians on in each act. Not only is *Rosencrantz* about two characters caught up in a play, with parallels to the human situation (is someone 'watching'? is a logic at work?) but acting itself is examined. The Tragedians show why theatre was banned under the Puritans, and why anxieties are felt today about what's available on video: at worst the actor's craft can degenerate into sadistic pornography, and an audience into voyeurs. Yet the Tragedians have real skill (we are told, p. 75/83, that they can even die 'from a great height': a pity we miss that one). Guil feels *'fear, vengeance, scorn'* (p. 114/123 – a revealing stage-note) at such claims to act death: but when in fury he stabs the Player, he is clearly taken in by the feigned death that follows. Like Hamlet watching the First Player weep and turn pale, Guil cannot tell the appearance from the reality; which is worrying for us all because we constantly make deductions about reality from appearances.

Death

This is only one of many topics in *Hamlet*, but is highlighted in Stoppard's title. As his Player says, Elizabethan tragedy demanded plenty of bodies at the end: 'a slaughterhouse – eight corpses all told' (p. 75/83); and it is significant that whereas the travelling actors in Shakespeare are equally happy to perform 'tragedy, comedy, history, pastoral', they become in Stoppard specialist Tragedians, for whom 'Blood is compulsory' (p. 24/33). Dying is their stock in trade.

Rosencrantz omits Shakespeare's late scene in which Hamlet talks with gravediggers merrily chucking up old skulls. Hamlet's comments, as Renaissance man, are mainly on the vanity of human aspirations: a skull might be that of a lawyer who specialised in purchases of land, but now ironically it is the 'fine dirt' itself which fills his 'fine pate'. Earlier ('To be or not to be') Hamlet says that he would not fear death if he could be sure it meant extinction, but that he dreads continuing consciousness, in some 'undiscovered country' of purgatory or hell. Yet 400 years later, after a major shift in beliefs, extinction rather than an after-life is the commoner fear; and in this respect Ros and Guil are entirely modern.

Unlike us, however, they are characters in a classic play, and on p. 76/84 find themselves watching their fate enacted in front of them. Stoppard's title goes further, implying that they were dead even at the start. There is a tension here between the fear of mortality and the horror of being immortal within art – the horror felt by the characters of Pirandello and, by implication, Beckett. A spun coin always comes down the same way, there is no wind and considerable doubt about the direction of the sun, and the fact that Ros and Guil can remember nothing before they were needed by the story suggests that they exist only for its purposes (but therefore *must* always exist for its purposes). There is still a hint of this at the end (p. 117: 'we'll know better next time' – we doubt if they will); though the predominant mood of the closing pages is more conventionally human: death is 'the endless time of never coming back'.

Reasoning

Jumpers, Stoppard's next major play, is about a philosopher; and already in *Rosencrantz* the main characters show a relish for the activity of logical reasoning. Philosophy is a serious business, trying to clarify the most fundamental questions of belief and perception; but it often approaches them by apparent playfulness – simplified or fanciful examples similar to Guil's unicorn story (pp. 11–12/21). We know nothing of Ros and Guil's lives outside the play – for the very good reason that they don't *have* them – but we can see that both men are by nature questioners, who want to puzzle things out. Guil is the more abstract and intellectually minded, Ros earthier (see him on toenails, on p. 9/18, or utterly ignoring Guil's unicorn story, p. 12/21). But both long to get a mental grip on their situation, as is seen in their respective attempts to sum things up on pp. 102–103: it makes them feel better to do so.

Almost as soon as the play begins (pp. 2–3/12–13) Guil is trying to assess their situation in terms of supposed mathematical 'laws' (probability, averages, diminished returns; in fact these are all popular myths). On p. 6/16 he draws up a 'list of possible explanations' and on pp. 6–7/17 offers mock-'syllogisms', a term from logic (see this book, p. 45). On p. 11/21 he goes into his unicorn story and on p. 51/60 the one about the Chinese philosopher. And so on: even Ros knows the philosophers' term '*non sequitur*' (p. 35/42), and is ironically (shamefacedly?) accused by Guil of applying logic (p. 102/111). Stoppard's first success identified him as a writer interested in the games philosophers play, and one early critic (who also made the mistake of taking the play as deathly serious, and grumbling about its jokes) even described him as 'a philosophy graduate'.

Characters

Rosencrantz is clearly not a play about subtle inter-personal relationships between richly drawn characters.

All Stoppard's early work tends towards comic cartoon, dominated by grotesque situations and the brilliantly worded bubbles coming out of people's heads. In later years, most strikingly in *Arcadia*, he has shown that he can, when he chooses, create skilful and rapid art-work of a psychologically realistic kind; but as late as 1978 he was still saying 'character doesn't really interest me very much'. If the characters in *Rosencrantz* seem less fully rounded and well-known to us than those in *Eastenders*, or even the principal figures in *Hamlet*, that's because Stoppard is aiming for something different.

The most obvious thing to note about Ros and Guil is that they are Elizabethan gentlemen only in appearance. Apart from a gag about the 'fashionable theory' of the earth going round the sun (p. 116/125) no attempt at all is made to link their mental processes to the Renaissance world of corrupt grandeur in which they have roles to play. They are walking anachronisms, though not as garish as the later beach umbrella – they don't talk about motor-bikes or movies, but psychologically they think and feel like members of the modern audience. Both the humour and the darkness of Stoppard's play derive substantially from this blending of ancient and modern.

Ros and Guil are also more defined as individuals than Shakespeare's interchangeable Rosencrantz and Guildenstern. Theatrically, they needed to be: they are centre-stage virtually throughout their play, and although the main drama is about their *common* situation, there had to be some tension between them, if only at the level of a comic double-act. Such double-acts (almost always male, and probably somewhere on your TV this week) typically present an image of irritated but long-term friendship, almost like a marriage. One is sharp-witted, or at least imagines he is; the other more of a numbskull, though sometimes his may be the final victory. One may be fat, the other thin; or they are tall and short; but the essential basic for comedy, as for drama of any kind, is that they must differ.

Stoppard's theatrical instinct transformed Shakespeare's bland courtiers, not quite into straight-man and idiot, but into a cerebral Guil (thinking more abstractly, trying to reason beyond his direct experience) and a more down-to-earth Ros. After Guil has spent two pages playing at abstract philosophy (pp. 7–8/17–18), Ros is more interested in his toenails. Ros is not a fool, but of the two he is the more easily fooled (e.g., by the Player, p. 54/63) and he prefers to get back to basics, even if they include a very basic fear of death (pp. 62–3/70–71). He is also the nicer of the two (p. 6/15). Stoppard has spoken of them as

> carrying out a dialogue which I carry out with myself. One of them is fairly intellectual, fairly incisive; the other one is thicker, nicer in a curious way, more sympathetic. (*In Conversation: Giles Gordon.*)

In their reactions to the letter ordering the death of Hamlet they anticipate later Stoppard work in which cleverness (especially with words) is opposed to natural innocence. Guil's sweetly reasonable speech excusing them from doing anything about it (pp. 101–102/110-11) anticipates Archie in *Jumpers*. But, mostly, Guil is decent. Unlike other double-act straight-men, he takes no joy in scoring points off his partner, if only because he feels their joint situation is too worrying for that; he is, rather, always the one trying to *interpret* their situation. He can be exasperated by Ros (pp. 60, 85/68, 93) but also concerned and gentle ('*nursemaid*', p. 29/38, '*quietly*', p. 39/47).

Guil is disgusted by the Players, whereas Ros is more earthily tempted. This may be partly because in Guil they cause '*fright*' (p. 17/27) – a fear for his own self-control or dignity? – but his compassion for Alfred (pp. 22–3) is clear enough. Finally, Guil is not only the more intellectual, he is also a stagey poet, letting his voice ring and sob in a series of speeches (pp. 4–5, 7–8, 17–18, 30, 86, 104, 116/14, 17–18, 27, 38–9, 94, 112, 125) which have been understandably described as 'kitsch' (cheap and false) but which are all part of the play's theatricality. 'On the wind of a windless day' ... 'our names shouted in a certain dawn' ... 'Yesterday was blue, like smoke.'

This 'ham' poetry is similar to that developed in the central speech of the Player (pp. 55–6/64), where it is more obviously appropriate and where Guil himself gives it the ironical slow clap. The Player is the only substantial 'character' in the play after Ros and Guil, and this showman fallen on hard times has been given a sharpness which keeps him mentally up to pace with them. The Player is equally at home either side of the looking-glass; he belongs in the Elizabethan play and understands its attitudes, yet he can speak with Ros and Guil in the voice of an aging actor-manager from the provincial repertory circuit of the first half of the twentieth century. He can discuss with them (and the audience) the nature of dramatic spectacle, the experience in which everyone there in the theatre is involved. Above all he is a supremely confident character, where Ros and Guil feel desperately insecure; jarringly confident (for the audience as well as the attendant lords) about the fact that 'most things end in death'.

He is not Shakespeare's First Player, who is an honest professional at the height of his powers. This Player has few moral scruples; his standing on the coin (p. 25/34) may be merely amusing, but his exploitation of Alfred is not (least of all when it's the Player's barrel that Alfred emerges from, p. 106/114). But both dramatists use their Players to explore the relationship of acting to reality. In Shakespeare (end of Act II, scene ii) Hamlet, acting mad because everyone round him also seems to be acting, is alarmed by the brilliant feigning of the First Player, who turns pale and weeps with entirely simulated grief. Stoppard's Ros and Guil, half-aware they're in a play but far from happy about it, are confronted by the hardened theatricality of the Tragedians, who know that they only exist when an audience sees them, and never question the script ('*Decides? It is written.*' p. 72/80).

A note on the Shakespearean roles in the play. Some productions have turned these into grotesque caricatures, or even puppets. It's an obvious temptation, but to yield to it is to make Ros and Guil also ridiculous. The text carefully avoids it; the stage-directions on p. 70/98, for example, are appropriate enough for this telescoped version, where Ophelia may understandably wail and totter; the instructions '*quiet edge*' and '*quick clipped sentence*' seem genuine notes for actors. The scraps of *Hamlet* should look like a conventional but uninspired performance: the action has to be serious enough for Ros and Guil to be convincingly caught up in it, but not so interesting that it distracts us from their predicament. The only points at which Stoppard allows himself to travesty *Hamlet* are in Act Three, where there is no Shakespearean action; and some may feel that even these – the beach umbrella (p. 90/99) and the spitting (p. 108/116) – slightly damage the play's consistency.

Stagecraft

Like a number of twentieth-century dramatists, Stoppard entertains partly by making us highly conscious of the experience, of the playing we have consented to witness. The parallelism between theatre and life itself is discussed above, pp. 28–9; but out interest in that parallel would not carry us through the evening; we are also talking showbiz, and the play itself must be skilfully made. The main effects of *Rosencrantz* could probably be achieved within half an hour; and the text we are studying is both an expansion of earlier material and one which could be ruthlessly cut. I have seen an amateur version reduced to one act (though probably without Stoppard's approval) and his own film-script is said to use less than half the original dialogue. We can be realistic about this; we are not dealing with scripture divinely inspired.

Rosencrantz follows Beckett and many 1950s radio-comedy writers in openly highlighting its need to fill up time. The audience is teased for having paid money to come here at all (and indeed some have walked out in disgust). In *Waiting for Godot* the underlying implication is nevertheless that anything else they might have done would have been equally pointless. Perhaps their time might even be better passed here, where at least there is a story to follow.

Rosencrantz has, however, far richer material than Beckett's play. To his original brilliant notion of following Ros and Guil in and out of Shakespeare's play, Stoppard then added a further idea almost better still – adapting Shakespeare's travelling players into go-betweens, who link the fixed course of the classic play with the modern speech and concerns of Ros and Guil, and can also provoke thoughts about theatre itself. Stoppard is thus able to ring the changes on three different kinds of action: the duologues of Ros and Guil; their interplay with the Player and Tragedians; and the fragments of *Hamlet*.

He uses every scene from Shakespeare in which R. and G. appear, except the by-play with a recorder (III. ii. 270ff) – though words of Hamlet in that scene mysteriously find their way into Guil's mouth on p. 104. The story of *Hamlet* maps out a clear course for this play, and a well-known one; the funny and disturbing scenes are of course Stoppard's, yet as we sit in the audience we are always looking forward to the next scrap of Shakespeare to see how it will be handled.

Initially the play follows the structure of *Waiting for Godot*: two men with nothing to do, trying to work out why they're here, eventually interrupted by distant sounds drawing nearer (an elementary theatrical trick: the audience strains to hear, and is quickened with anticipation) and then by what Beckett's Vladimir calls 'reinforcements' (in the task of getting through the evening). This pattern is exactly repeated in Stoppard's third act: just when the duologue is flagging, the recorder is heard again; and in Act Two the Player also enters at a comparable point, though he arrives via Shakespeare.

Stoppard holds back his third option, the action of *Hamlet*, till relatively late in Act One. It's an effective delay, making us enjoyably impatient to see how, if indeed at all, Shakespeare will be used; meanwhile the duologue, and then the interaction with the Tragedians, can be well established. The delay also paces the arrival of the vital scene in which R. and G. interrogate Hamlet: this can then begin as we break up for the first interval, and end as we return, giving the strong and important impression that the action of *Hamlet* is going on, offstage, continuously.

There is far more of *Hamlet* in Act Two, coming relatively fast and furious, and less of the double-act (which will need to fill much of Act Three). Act Two – and indeed the whole play – pivots round the 'dress rehearsal' (pp. 69–75/76–82), which is brilliantly crafted. The dumbshow to be performed in front of Claudius suddenly takes on a life of its own (p. 74/80) and develops into a dumbshow of the further action of *Hamlet*, in which the audience perceives (though they themselves apparently don't) that Ros and Guil are doomed. The blackout (p. 77/84) then takes us on to the premature end of 'The Murder of Gonzago', curtailed by Claudius; after which the dead likenesses of Ros and Guil rise and prove now to be Ros and Guil themselves, still alive though still doomed. These few pages have been the most exciting in the whole play, both in their melodramatic material and in the overlapping of different dramas. Now, from here on, Stoppard's play must surely be gradually – and appropriately – running down.

The idea of a third act seems problematic. The last line of Act Two – 'anything could happen yet' – may at first seem merely a feeble curtain-line. But Ros is expressing a *hope* (he doesn't want to believe that his fate is already determined). And as for the dramatist, he is reminding us that he is now out on his own. We have now passed the last point in *Hamlet* at which R. and G. are seen; we are out of the Shakespearean shipping lanes and into uncharted seas – we are, indeed, on a boat. This does involve some damage to the previous elegant idea that Ros and Guil are unable to leave the stage; clearly, at the end of Act Two they have to. Stoppard contrives the change of rules deftly enough, however, with Ros's line (p. 87/95) 'He *said* we can go.' Hamlet in fact *told* them to go; but Ros's 'can' is ambiguous: perhaps Hamlet has freed them from a spell and they are now capable of going.

The Shakespearean basis for Act Three is minimal: events merely summarised by Hamlet on his return, and including one shameless piece of plot-forcing, the attack by pirates which enables Hamlet to change ships. That at least Stoppard feels licensed to mock, in a piece of Goon or Blackadder-ish action on p. 109/117–18 (after a previous distinct echo of Goon-dom on p. 89/98). The other bit of Shakespearean plot is the letter to the English king, which Hamlet discovers and alters to order the deaths of R. and G. By allowing Ros and Guil to discover it first, Stoppard raises the possibility that they might in some way disrupt the predetermined course of things, but makes it also a moment of moral choice, the first they have ever had. Ros wants to save Hamlet, Guil dissuades him. If Ros's better moral instinct had prevailed, who knows? – perhaps, after all, the fixed plan might have been broken. If they had warned Hamlet of the contents of the letter, he would presumably have been grateful, would not have substituted their names, and the line 'Rosencrantz and Guildenstern are dead' would never have been spoken.

It is a fine touch, from a dramatist whose later plays will often feature moral choices. The other device which energises Act Three departs entirely from Shakespeare:

the re-introduction of the Tragedians, with a passable explanation of why they urgently stowed away on a ship. 'Pleased to see us?' asks the Player (p. 106/114). He gets no response; Guil, in particular, has always been hostile to him. And the Player's apparent warmth vanishes when the rewritten letter is read out (pp. 113–14/122). Now the Tragedians '*form a casually menacing circle*'; if the script says Ros and Guil are to die, that's it, die they must.

It's still impossible to see how Stoppard can end his play: there will have to be some kind of fudge. And so indeed there is, but it's brilliantly appropriate: Guil's attack on the Player (first verbal, then physical) brings together in a climax two long-running themes: death, and the nature and ethics of theatrical illusion. An actor gives a convincing rendering of death in agony. We in the audience know it is only acting; but it is acting of the one event which can never have been personally experienced. Theatre often plays out things that frighten or disturb us, but Ancient Greek and neo-classical French drama refused to allow this feigning of death on stage. The argument for and against allowing it goes on in our stomachs as we watch. Since in this case the actor is acting a Player who has previously boasted that his team can die 'heroically, comically, ironically, slowly, suddenly, disgustingly, charmingly, or from a great height,' we are also unsure whether he is acting death, or only acting a Player acting death.

It partly depends whose reaction we watch. If we watch Guil's, he is sure he has killed the Player, and so is Ros; if we watch the Tragedians, we see on their faces only 'interest'. So theatre shows us different reactions, which become different versions of the event. If Guil has 'really' killed the Player, it is instantly significant in several ways:

it means the Tragedians are wrong this time, the deceivers deceived (that'll teach them to muck about with death); it means the intellectual, fastidious Guil has committed murder; and above all it means he has successfully interfered in the proposed destiny of himself and the Tragedians within the play of *Hamlet*. (Or perhaps he has not: because within *that* play none of them is needed any more.)

The theatre is tensely still after the body has ceased to move. Very faintly, though our intellects immediately reject it, we recognise the astronomically remote possibility that the actor is genuinely dead (the idea is used in several classic detective stories including one called *Hamlet, Revenge!*). Much more credibly, within Stoppard's play Guil may really have killed the Player; something of this kind happens at the end of Pirandello's play. Then the Tragedians begin to applaud enthusiastically, and for a second we are flooded with embarrassment, not yet certainly for ourselves but possibly for them, because the Player may not get up. And then of course he does, and we feel the more thoroughly fooled ourselves. Immediately, as if mercilessly, the Player then directs a cavalcade of violent deaths, apparently mocking us in the audience and also, of course, mocking the undying Ros and Guil. Yet this time the Tragedians, we gradually and very cautiously sense, are 'really' dying. The deaths are compelling in themselves, and they also include (for the second time, the first being on p. 76/84) those of the Spies wearing the same cloaks as Ros and Guil ... who, like us in the audience, remain watching.

This is *theatre*. Call it pretence or trickery or fooling about, it is a special kind of shared excitement which at the very least passes an evening and at most can feel as profound as religious ritual. The student working at home on the mere text of a play has to make a conscious and repeated effort not to undervalue this live event, which is richer not only than the printed page, but also than film or video. It is always a gathering of human beings, performers as well as audience, in one place together.

Textual Notes

Act One

1/1   *a place without any visible character* – scenery of any kind would suggest a distinct place, with a before and after – the kind of recognisable reality Ros and Guil keep hoping to latch on to. Instead they are in an Absurdist limbo.

   – *character note* – Stoppard departs from the faceless interchangeability of Shakespeare's Rosencrantz and Guildenstern. Ros doesn't think abstractly about the long sequence of 'heads', just about his friendship. But Guil is '*worried by the implications*' – which he explores in the next few pages.

2/2   There is an art to the building up of suspense – Guil may seem to step out of character here, to tease an uneasy audience and make them laugh. But at a realist level this is also Guil trying not to panic – see his character note on p. 1 – and making a nervous joke to Ros.

   – *has nowhere to go ... examining the confines of the stage* – gradually it will appear that Guil and Ros are unable to leave the stage (having no existence beyond it?).

3/13 law of diminishing returns – Like Guil's earlier
'laws' – of probability and averages – this is
not a scientific law at all, just a popular
perception or belief. The longer the 'heads' go
on, the less Guil and Ros can find the 'energy'
to be surprised, or even bother to spin the next.

4/14 I'm relieved ... spun coins! – Guil is slightly
reassured by this glimpse of normal (as it were,
realistic) self-interest in the trusting Ros. He
touches and pulls him closer, and wants to
insist that they have a past together. But 'as
long as I remember ... I forget' (a joke more or
less instantly repeated on p. 7/16) is consistent
with their having no past at all, outside their
play.

5/15 fear? ... (In fury ...) – Guil is exasperated and
alarmed at Ros's failure to see any implications.

6/15 I'm afraid it is – his one day, for his transitory
theatrical usefulness.

6/16 possible explanations – Guil longs for
intellectual control.

– children of Israel – protected by God, in
Judaeo-Christian scripture, whereas God
condemned Lot's wife (to become an unmoving
fixity).

– syllogism – in philosophy, a basic format for
logical argument, often (as in the two nonsense
versions on this page) in three statements: two
premises and a conclusion.

7/17 wheels at Ros and raps out – he needs to
awaken Ros to the 'implications'.

– The scientific approach ... – Guil persists in
trying to reason like a philosopher (attempting

to analyse experience dispassionately and without 'panic'). 'Postulate' is a term from philosophy meaning 'claim as true for the sake of this argument'.

8/18 fortuitous – happening by chance; 'ordained' – predestined.

– after death ... But you're not dead – a deceptively light-hearted introduction to the topic which will loom over the play.

9/18 I cut my fingernails ... And yet ... toenails – these are contradictory experiences, but both suggest non-time, a lack of past or future.

10/20 Which way ... direction – they are in a place of no geography, with no future to go to (*do we*) or past arrived from (*did we*). A pun then develops on *direction*.

11/20 demolish – Guil sets an imaginary philosophical problem.

11/21 A man ... a deer – again a kind of thought-experiment from philosophy. The un-, sub- or supernatural sight is most alarming when there are two witnesses (and Ros and Guil are two). When there are many we feel reassured, though Guil, in a thoroughly twentieth-century caution, still sees 'reality' as only 'the name we give' it.

In Stoppard's early plays, strange occurrences often prove to have rational explanations (see discussion in this book, p. 13–14). But note here the final reverse twist, where the extraordinary ('horse with an arrow in its forehead') is mistaken for the humdrum ('deer'). 'Recites' may suggest yet another twist: is the crowd itself deluded, saying what it has been trained to say?

12/21   Halt! – the Players arrive at the corresponding point at which Pozzo and Lucky arrive (again heralded by noises off) in *Waiting for Godot*. The meta-theatre joke in Beckett (Pozzo and Lucky helping to pass time for those stuck on stage) is here more or less reversed (those on stage are the audience the Players need).

13/22   Tumblers – acrobats; 'tumble' – sexual romp.

  – Guildenstern ... Rosencrantz – Shakespeare himself seems to have set up this confusion (see p. 26/35), perhaps to suggest the falseness of interchangeable cardboard spies. In Stoppard it becomes both funny and pathetic: even their own identity feels uncertain. Note, however, '*without embarrassment*': they are behaving like actors gradually getting into their parts, and it's a perfectly normal problem in theatre circles to be unable to remember which of these two lords is which.

  – Don't clap too loudly – a similar music-hall joke occurs in John Osborne's *The Entertainer*.

14/23   dénouements – conclusions of plots.
    flagrante delicto – caught in the act.

15/24   A nest of children – this is paraphrased from Shakespeare, where it was a genuine topical reference.

  – There's one born every minute – meaning, one idiot: the Player is disgruntled that Ros has failed to pick up his sexual hint ('stoop ... bent'). But of course the line makes literal sense referring back to the 'children'.

16/25 Chance ... fate – compare p. 8/18: 'the fortuitous and the ordained'.

17/26 caught up in the action – the Player instantly assumes that Guil is showing interest in pornography ('You're quicker than your friend'), but in fact Guil's mind is running more on the unknown function that awaits him and Ros: he is looking for some guide or pointer.

– It could have been ... – see the last note. Guil feels 'rage' because he expected better than this; and 'fright' because he may not get it (and also his violence to the Player suggests he may feel sexually threatened).

18/27 *resumes the struggle* – though the theatre audience never sees this stage direction, and here it simply refers to Alfred's movements, the words come from the very first lines of *Waiting for Godot*, where they mean the decision to continue with life itself.

22/31 Was it for this? – compare 'It could have been' on p. 18/27. Also an echo of Wilfred Owen's poem 'Futility', on a dead young soldier: 'Was it for this the clay grew tall?'

23/32 You and I, Alfred ... – Guil seems to be thinking that he and Alfred could simply walk out now. This play would then fold; so would *Hamlet* and the play within it in which Alfred is due to act. But the word *could* means they won't; and one reason is that Guil by now realises they *couldn't*. Alfred's sniffle, however, suggests that he fears Guil has in mind some new sexual abuse.

- -cide – killing; 'matri', etc: mother, father, brother, wife and (after Ros's pun) self.
- vice versa – (with a pun on 'vice') gods hoping to capture maidenheads.

24/33 rhetoric – elaborate speeches.

- we'll let you know – the traditional line of dismissal to actors who have auditioned.
- Thirty-eight! – Ros hopes this is some Kama-Sutra-like sexual position, but it's simply a players' code, such as might be called in rugby or American football.

25/34 *immobility* – Stoppard here tricks his audience. The previous pages have accustomed us to Ros and Guil's inability to leave the stage, with grim hints of predestination, and at first here we seem to be getting more of the same. But the Player turns out not to be suffering from any such condition: he's merely a crook.

26/35 *Hamlet, with his doublet* – here we see onstage a scene which is offstage in Shakespeare, where it is described by Ophelia in the words which make up most of the stage-direction here.

- Welcome, dear Rosencrantz – the speeches from here to the top of p. 29/38 come accurately from Shakespeare; but the stage directions are Stoppard's own mischievous choreography.

27/36 During the '*Fractional suspense*', the Queen decides not to risk repeating her husband's muddle of their names. On p. 28/36–7 Ros and Guil themselves get caught out.

29/38 *high* and dry – at last, with huge relief, Guil arrives at the usual word-pairing. The previous attempts represent both their faltering grip on

    everything, and also a typically Stoppardian
    mockery of cliché.

- 'wife' ... 'house' – these words seem to come
  haphazardly to Guil's mind, but they remind us
  what fundamental information we lack about
  these two characters. (Do they perhaps also
  lack it themselves?)

30/39 a grotesque – a weird person.

- Consistency is all I ask! – as a director might of
  his actors, perhaps. This starts a series of
  similar patterned exclamations, each with
  rhyming partner; others are on pp. 37 and 93/
  45 and 102.

- our daily mask – as stage characters, rather
  than people.

32/41 amnesiac – suffering from loss of memory.

- Elephantine – legendarily, elephants never
  forget.
  retainer – at court meant a servant; so Guil has
  got into a twist.

- Words, words – from *Waiting for Godot*, where
  it is a shortened quotation from *Hamlet*; so the
  wheel of reference comes full circle.

- A short, blunt human pyramid – obviously, this
  is taking 'constructive' far too literally, and
  with only two of them it would be extremely
  'short' and 'blunt'. Yet six years later Stoppard
  demanded an actual human pyramid, early in
  Jumpers.

33/42 The idea of the questions game is borrowed
    from *Next Time I'll Sing to You* (1963) by
    Stoppard's friend James Saunders. There the
    analogy is with cricket; here, the tennis term

'love' is used. Many of the questions have obvious ironic significance in Ros and Guil's situation.

34/42 rhetoric – here means questions that can't reasonably expect an answer. (In Saunders: 'the bowling of rhetorical questions ... shall constitute a no-ball.')

35/43 *non-sequitur* – means 'it doesn't follow logically'.

36/45 *Triumph dawns* – because Ros answered rightly to his name.

37/46 How do you know? – in Shakespeare, they are supposed to have known Hamlet for years, but here Guil only seems to know what he has just been told (p. 27/35) about Hamlet's 'transformation'.

39/47 You've forgotten – Ros is supposed to be practising 'gleaning' information from Hamlet. Challenged, Ros reverts to their previous confusion, and promptly gets that wrong too. *hypothesis* – (here) imaginary situation.

41/49 Let me ... king – this is a more or less accurate summary of the background in Shakespeare. Usurpation – illegally seizing a throne.

44/53 How dost thou Guildenstern? – again the words are Shakespeare's, the stage directions Stoppard's. And they move offstage for the scene which is onstage in Shakespeare.

Act Two

46/55 The whole text until Hamlet and Polonius's exit is Shakespeare's. Hamlet shows himself far from mad; he bids a courteous welcome–

back and goodbye-for-now to R. and G., and asks them not to take offence if he welcomes the Players more heartily. He is a shrewd, polished prince in a devious court where hints are everything: even as he gracefully apologises for his coolness, he leaves R. and G. in no doubt that it is consciously intended.

– but mad north north-west – only a touch 'off' (i.e. not seriously mad).

– handsaw – (possibly) a heron.

47/57 Again, Stoppard's onstage scene begins as Shakespeare's goes offstage.

48/57 Half of what he said . . . – a more or less fair description of how in *Hamlet* he does indeed tease them, as well as being a joke about the linguistic difficulty of Shakespeare for today's audiences.

50/58 Pragmatism – a practical approach; this is another of Guil's semi-philosophical terms. He of course knows they are unable to go anywhere, even to 'have a look'.

50/59 *Draught*, yes – actors often complain that stages are draughty places.

51/59 It's what we're counting on – i.e. to keep the play going: another Godot-like joke. But 'Ultimately' (with its faint suggestion of the end of the world, a Last Judgement, etc.) makes it sound much more portentous.

51/60 If we start being arbitrary . . . lost – this briefly and lightly glances at theological debate in which free will ('arbitrary' here means independent, on our own initiative) is set against predestination.

- Perhaps even decisions which seem to us spontaneous are actually predetermined (by Fate or God or – some might think today – our genes); if so, we are 'lost' in hopes of being able to act independently.
- Envy him – this is a fierce twist. The philosopher's uncertainty might seem to make him unenviably insecure; but he does at least have a choice between two clear identities, whereas Guil and Ros (and perhaps we ourselves?) can be sure of none.
- Fire! – yelling *Fire!* in a theatre is a traditional example of where 'free speech' should be restricted.

53/62 The speeches as far as 'Good, my Lord' are from *Hamlet*, and crucial to its plot.

54/62 dumbshows – a mime summarising the play to follow. See pp. 69–76/76–83.

55/63 that somebody is *watching* – obviously this makes sense to fellow-actors, but it's also a passing reference to a view in philosophy (and incidentally some twentieth-century physics) that something doesn't exist or happen till it is observed.

thirty-eight? – see note on p. 24/33.

56/64 if these eyes could weep! – primarily, Guil is mocking the Player's 'camp' or 'kitsch' style, as in 'silent on the road to Elsinore.' But, secondly, does Guil, as a 'character' with a scripted role in a play, have enough personality or freedom to 'weep'?

- with a vengeance ... figure of speech – revenge is the central topic of *Hamlet*.

57/65 Escapism! – this is the charge often levelled by 'social realists' at literary subject-matter comfortably distant from the audience's own problems. But in this case a King and Queen will indeed be the audience.

– the wind is blowing ... two levels – see p. 50/59.

58/67 honoured – a faint hint here of the moral insistence of Stoppard's later plays. Even in a state of uncertainty we should endeavour to trust and be trustworthy.

61/69 Next! – the cry to actors waiting for audition: come on stage and do your stuff. A running joke develops: Ros demanding more professional support to keep the action going ('Come out talking!' ... 'taking us for granted,' pp. 63–4/71–2) but then instantly objecting when it arrives (p. 65/73; 'public park', p. 67–75).

63/71 to death! – as in, 'with a vengeance' on p. 56, Guil's cliché is over-appropriate.

– yet! ... Schmarsus ... already – caricature Jewish forms of speech. (The Jew Saul changed his name to Paul when converted to Christianity.)

– Blue, red – either of these would be standard before 'in the face'; but 'green' isn't. Guil frequently seems cast as straight-man, correcting a dimmer Ros.

– Silverstein! ... Abdullah – Silverstein is a Jewish name; Abdullah a Moslem one. The idea of eternity seems to have set Ros's mind running vaguely on religious conversion (possibly because it might bring salvation?), but we never know how this story might have developed, nor the one started at the botttom of the page.

64/72 Did he receive you well? ... Affront Ophelia ... – these lines are Shakespeare's.

66/74 *weighing up the pros and cons* ... – in other words, Hamlet is at this moment murmuring to himself the most famous soliloquy in all drama, 'To be or not to be'; not the ideal time for Ros to 'accost him' with 'Now look here, what's it all about ...' (See Guil's comment on p. 67/74: 'I thought your direct informal approach was going to stop this thing dead in its tracks.')

– *No point in looking* – Ros muddles two proverbial sayings: 'never look a gift horse in the mouth' and 'don't move till you see the whites of its eyes'.

67/75 I'm not going to stand for it ... Guess who?! – Ros is determined to interrupt the action of *Hamlet*, which is ignoring him.

68/76 Stop picking your nose – in Jean Genet's *The Balcony*, a Queen is described picking her nose. The line about 'cerebral process ... blood' occurs also in Stoppard's novel, *Lord Malquist and Mr Moon*.

70/77 *The mime* – the dumbshow is from Shakespeare – and the debate about its function is an old one in literary criticism. Pages 69–70/77 jumble together different bits of Shakespeare, including some of his directions for the mime.

72/80 It is *written* – as if foretold (predestined) in ancient scripture.

– The bad ... means – a twist of Oscar Wilde's lines in *The Importance of Being Earnest*, themselves a parody of Victorian moralising: 'The good ended happily, and the bad unhappily. That is what Fiction means.'

73/80   good story ... mirror life – basic traditional theories for drama, the first vaguely based on Aristotle, the second echoing words of Hamlet himself ('hold the mirror up to nature').

73/81   It's all the same to me – literally true: the Player has no life separate from art. (Nor, we are pretty sure by now, do Ros and Guil.)

– The mime now becomes a dumbshow of *Hamlet* itself; the Player still speaks of 'Lucianus' but the story told is more or less Hamlet's.

74/81   *oedipal* – son in love with mother, as in the Oedipus legend.

– two smiling ... spies – the Player's apparent struggle to find the right words allows him ironic stage-business at the expense of Ros and Guil, who remain unaware.

74/82   hoist by their own petard? – the phrase (meaning 'blown up by their own bomb') comes from *Hamlet*.

75/83   a long time since ... when was it? – not only does Ros fail to recognise his own coat, he is again fumbling for a past he does not have (compare pp. 5 and 7).

76/84   a sheep – or a lamb – English proverb: 'as well be hung for a sheep as for a lamb'.

– suspend one's disbelief – the phrase comes from S. T. Coleridge, who said that in a theatre things are obviously false, but the audience 'willingly' co-operates in this way. Here the twist, of course, is that it was in fact a uniquely *genuine* stage-occurrence.

77/85　it was light all the time, you see – Guil is now convinced of the fixity of his condition ('I've been taken in before'), but this time Stoppard has tricked him, since the light did indeed come up '*as a sunrise*'.

– They're waiting – Guil means the other characters, but it's true also of the audience, the view of which Ros has just found vaguely familiar.

– Good old east – Edward Albee's *The Zoo Story* has the line 'Good old north'.

78/86　*Small pause* – neither remembers his name being Guildenstern – which is perhaps the main reason for their '*desperation*'.

– seek him out – makes them hesitate for two reasons: (a) it sounds risky, if Hamlet is now killing people; (b) it would involve leaving the stage, but 'getting somewhere' (mid-p. 80/88, back in '*original positions*') is just what they seem unable to do.

82/89　Properly – they have been watching deaths acted by the Players.

80/90　Lord Hamlet! ... Bring in the lord – the spoken words are all from Shakespeare – but the farcical action is Stoppard's. This passage was not in his original version but was added after a suggestion by Laurence Olivier.

86/93　Good sir ... Fortinbras – the Hamlet–Soldier exchange is again from Shakespeare.
Meanwhile, Ros and Guil feel as if the seasons

of the year (and life?) are telescoping inwards –
from spring to autumn in ten lines.

87/95 He *said* we can go; anything could happen yet –
are discussed above, this book, p. 41.

Act Three

Here the play can no longer weave in and out of
Shakespeare's, since that doesn't include the events on
the boat (they are merely summarised by Hamlet himself
afterwards). This has led some critics to see Ros and
Guil as now free to choose their own future; but it seems
to me they are still trapped in the story of *Hamlet*.

89/98 it feels like my leg ... Dead – (a) a variant on the
old confusion over which of them is which; and
(b) a reminder of the title theme, which is now
increasingly dominant.

– We're on a boat – the pitch darkness means
that this act has so far resembled radio, and
here is a trick from the Goon Shows which the
schoolboy Stoppard enjoyed in the 1950s:
absurd excess of sound-clichés followed by this
Eccles-like perception.

90/99 *a gaudy striped umbrella* – suddenly Stoppard
allows himself one huge comic anachronism, a
joke he avoids elsewhere in the play though it
can tempt directors (one production ended with
music from an advertisement – 'happiness is a
cigar named Hamlet'). For the first time
Shakespeare's play seems to be mocked, and
perhaps diminished.

92/100 Where? ... disbelief – like a fooled child, Guil
looks around for 'Those eskimos'. His faculty

for mistrust has been exhausted in the first two acts.

93/101 *Guil licks a finger* – there still seems no clear wind direction. Front rows of the audience are relieved when he sends Ros the other way.

93/102 For those in peril on the sea – the refrain of a well-known hymn.

our daily cue – as characters in a play.

95/104 say something original! ... stagnant! – Stoppard waves his red rag closer than ever to the potentially infuriated bull (the audience). Compare *Waiting for Godot*: 'Nothing happens, nobody comes, nobody goes, it's awful.'

96/105 keep us going a bit – although Ros and Guil have by now accepted that they exist only for the story, they still want to 'live' in it as long as possible.

99/107 I don't believe in it anyway – compare p. 100/108, 'I have no confidence in England', p. 106/114, 'all right for England'; p. 112/121 'a dead end' – a series of laughs for British audiences (better still for the original Scottish audience!).

– clutching at ... drowning man – the hidden proverb which has tripped Ros up is 'You can't make bricks without straw.'

100/109 (*angrily*) Let me finish – for once (because he is playing a king) Ros has become the dominant one – and Guil doesn't like it.

101/110 We're his *friends* – i.e., we can't possibly let him go to his death. Throughout the play Ros has tended to show the 'average man's' reactions, where Guil is cleverer and more

cerebral. Stoppard's later work, for example
Jumpers, often pits instinctive human decency
against intellectual amorality: 'you can persuade
a man of anything if he is clever enough', and
Guil's long speech ('Well, yes, and then again
no') shows him persuading *himself*, resisting
(see following speeches) both logic and justice.

– You've only got their word for it – Ros and
Guil have no memory of any such 'young days'.
The script tells them all they know.

102/110 Socrates – Ancient Greek philosopher.
'Philosophically' is therefore a sort of pun,
Guil's main meaning being the popular one of
accepting life's ups and downs.

– assuming you were in character – a standard
reassurance to actors covering up errors: keep
behaving as your character would, and the
audience will notice nothing. Of course Ros
and Guil have no option but to remain in
character.

104/112 governing ... eloquent music – extracted from
Hamlet showing a recorder to Guildenstern,
Hamlet III, ii.

105/114 Plausibility is all I ... – see note on p. 30: here
Ros begs for another theatre requirement,
offended by the notion that the Players may be
inside the barrels.

– *coda* – musical end-piece. This is the last of
these paired lines, and Guil's tone may suggest
everything running down.

– Call us ... tune – The proverb is 'Whoever pays
the piper calls the tune,' so Guil's line is
appropriate both to the pipe just heard and to

the idea that he has to perform in someone else's story.

106/114 *from the Player's barrel* – compare p. 22/31, 'Do you lose often, Alfred?'

108/116 without restriction. Within limits ... – this contradiction sums up their predicament, as does Hamlet's boomeranging spit three lines later – as if a glass wall confined all the characters within the play.

109/118 *The Pirates attack* – in Shakespeare this is a blatant plot-mechanism (to get Hamlet off the ship and back to Denmark): fair game for Stoppard's mockery.

– Action! – Hamlet here appears the most unheroic of 'heroes'. The disappearance of the barrel in which Ros and Guil hid momentarily suggests the play's title.

110/119 *not a pick up* – i.e., not referring to the Player's words, but to what may have happened to Hamlet. The word 'dead' presses more and more on our ears.

112/120 *ingratiating* – trying to win favour. Ros invents a bet Guil would be certain to win. Compare p. 94/103 'I wanted to make you happy.'

113/122 *double takes* – a standard trick of comedy; he belatedly understands (long after the audience) what he's just said.

114/122 contained within a larger one – compare note on p. 108/116.

115/123 *he pushes the blade in ...* – this seems to be Guil departing from any predetermined script, taking action of his own for the first time. And the audience should be fooled by the Player's

'death'. One critic even suggests that his
recovery is 'magic'; but surely the point is that
the dagger at the Player's belt is a collapsible
one, an ancient theatrical prop. That is the kind
of dagger *he* needs, since his whole existence is
onstage; and Guil's attempt at an independent
'plot' has failed.

115/124 cheated – by having a real dagger and thus
genuinely dying, instead of using his technique.
We perhaps remember the actor, p. 76/84,
whose genuine hanging wasn't convincing.

116/125 the fashionable theory – that the planets revolve
round the sun – a new and controversial idea to
Elizabethans.

117/126 next time – their play may be performed again
(but the audience knows they will never be free
to 'know better').

— Rosencrantz and Guildenstern are dead – the
entire play has been building up to its title line,
which we now hear in its Shakespearean
context. Originally, and much less strongly in
my view, Stoppard ended his play with a
messenger banging on a shutter all over again
(see p. 9/19).

Jumpers

In *Jumpers* Stoppard is trying, in his own words to *Theatre Quarterly*, 'to end up by contriving the perfect marriage between the play of ideas and farce or perhaps even high comedy'. A simpler starting-point may be to see it as a satire: that is, a comic story which holds up for ridicule some tendencies of its time. Satire is at heart serious, even angry; but it often uses the broadest comic tricks and traditions.

Jumpers satirises twentieth-century relativist thinkers – those who claim that there are no absolute values such as goodness, truth, or beauty, but simply the relative opinions of individuals depending on where they are 'coming from' and where they stand. If in fact they don't stand anywhere consistently, but keep always 'jumping' about, they can lose all moral sense. The play shows such relativism not only dominating the intellectual world of a university, but also taking over politically in a whole country.

Also satirised, however, is the central character, George, a philosopher who resists relativism. He persists in believing in altruism, the unselfish instinct to act for others' benefit. He is convinced that human beings have a moral conscience, and that beyond us is some sort of god. But George is an ineffectual person. He gets confused even on his own professional ground – in a lecture we hear him preparing – and he is unable to help his wife, Dotty, who is suffering a mental breakdown. She is, surprisingly, a

63

'prematurely-retired musical-comedy actress'. John Weightman (*Encounter*, April 1972) describes a TV chat-show in the late 1960s where the philosopher A. J. Ayer sat side by side with the sultry performer Eartha Kitt:

> That is, they were side by side to begin with, but Miss Kitt gradually edged in, absent-mindedly laid a tender palm on the Professor's knee and looked up into his face with calculated awe every time he uttered a long word ... Mr Stoppard saw this and said to himself ... 'Some day I can write a play about a philosopher and an actress: brain and gut.'

Dotty cracked up when men began to walk about on the moon. Something that had seemed to her always up there in the sky, a fixed remote certainty rather like one of George's absolute values, was suddenly merely another geographical surface, where 'the local idea of a sane action may well differ from ours' (p. 26/38).

Jumpers begins like a glitzy show, but is rapidly interrupted by a fatal gunshot. What follows is partly a whodunnit (never solved), but more about how the murder is covered up – an example of how relativism extended to its extremes might extinguish all moral principle. Yet more grief is shown for the deaths of a goldfish, a hare and a tortoise. The mode of the play is that of sharp cartoon, and the final scene is a crazy dream-like sequence; the overall style is a fierce 'sick' humour, only too appropriate to the cynical intellectual attitudes it attacks. Yet Stoppard has always spoke of *Jumpers* as 'serious' as well as 'funny', and it displays more of his own concerns than his first big success six years earlier, *Rosencrantz*.

To the student, *Jumpers* looks quite a challenge. It makes many glancing references to philosophy; but the good news is that it more or less explains them as far as is needed. This is not in itself a profound play: it is a satire about profound questions.

Ideally the student starts by watching a performance; second-best, by play-reading it aloud with others. In any case, the whole play should at first be taken fairly fast, for its comedy and its story. The synopsis below can then be used for revision; and it is followed by discussion of philosophical ideas in the play, of characterisation, and of stage-craft, as well as detailed page-by-page notes. But now is the moment, for a newcomer to the play, to put the present book down and turn to Stoppard's.

Synopsis

A sweeping British electoral victory has been won by the Radical Liberals. In the spacious flat of Dotty, a 'prematurely-retired musical-comedy actress', a celebratory party is held. George, her husband, remains in his study and even calls the police under a false name to complain about the noise. At the party a team of Jumpers (amateur gymnasts), all clad in Rad-Lib yellow, form a human pyramid. Suddenly one of them is shot dead (p. 5/21) from the shadows – conceivably by Dotty, who seems mentally unhinged. The party fades away and Dotty is left in her bedroom holding the dead Jumper, whose name was McFee. Her friend Archie tells her to keep the body out of sight till the morning.

Next morning (p. 7/22) a national holiday has been declared and a triumphal military procession is being held. At the same time on the moon (p. 8/23) two astronauts fight for the one place in their damaged space capsule. Selfishness is evidently in fashion. All these events are watched by Dotty on her television set. We later hear (pp. 24–5/36–7) that the Rad-Libs have taken over the broadcasting services and appointed their former spokesman on agriculture as the new Archbiship of Canterbury.

George remains unaware of the murder; the corpse is always hidden from his view whenever he enters the bedroom. He continues to work on his contribution to a forthcoming philosophical symposium: he is a professor of moral philosophy who still – unfashionably – defends his intuitions (instinctive feelings without evidence – gut feelings, we might say) of the existence of God and goodness. He is planning to enliven his lecture by the use of a bow and arrow (which he accidentally fires on p. 13/28), a hare and a tortoise.

Dotty stages charades for George to guess (pp. 16 and 31/30 and 42). Their relationship seems affectionate but she has refused to have sex with him since her mental breakdown (which was apparently – p. 27/38 – triggered by the moon landings). She is, however, repeatedly visited in her bedroom by Archie, who is a distinguished psychiatrist, the Vice-Chancellor of George's university (p. 19/33), and an exponent of Rad-Lib relativism (p. 29/41).

A police inspector, Bones, arrives. An anonymous phone call has alerted him to the murder, and he has come in person because he is a fan of Dotty's singing (p. 34/45). George believes Bones is merely there because of his own phone call about the noise, and amazes Dotty by saying he will take the blame (p. 41/50). While Bones is entranced by Dotty in her bedroom, George returns to his lecture (p. 44/52), attacking his expected opponent at the symposium, the Professor of Logic, McFee – and the audience remembers that McFee was the name of the Jumper shot dead in the first scene. At the end of Act One, unseen by Bones and George, Archie's Jumpers smuggle the corpse out in a plastic body-bag, moving in rhythm to a song sung by Dotty (p. 48/56).

At the start of Act Two, Bones assures George there is a body in the bedroom, but they find it gone. Instead (p. 54/60), within the curtained bed, Archie is applying intimate therapy to Dotty, using a machine which analyses skin sensations. George goes disgustedly back to work on his lecture. Archie introduces himself to the inspector by his full name: Sir Archibald Jumper. He begins negotiations with Bones (p. 59/62) to save Dotty from prosecution. Archie is a lawyer and a coroner as well as everything else, and his version will be that McFee shot himself in a public park, where the body was found by a team of amateur gymnasts. This is what he also tells George (p. 65/68). Back in the bedroom he comes upon Bones, blacked-up and in drag for a charade, and threatens to disclose what he has seen if Bones fails to co-operate (p. 68).

George has lost his hare and Dotty fools him into believing she is eating it for lunch (p. 74/76). George grumbles about this to the caretaker, Crouch, but they are at cross-purposes and Crouch believes George is saying that Dotty is eating McFee (p. 76/77). Crouch reveals that it was he who telephoned the police about the murder, and finally George learns what happened (p. 76/77). Meanwhile, Crouch reads George's lecture and shows himself to be a keen amateur philosopher, the result of a friendship with Professor McFee. What is more (p. 80/80) McFee was having an affair with George's Secretary but was too terrified of her possible reaction to admit he was already married. Crouch also discloses that McFee had been so disgusted by the astronauts fighting on the moon that he had suddenly swung round to a belief in altruism, decided to enter a monastery and revealed all to the Secretary. Now it seems likely that it was she, infuriated, who fired the shot which killed him, but Archie insists we shall never know for certain. He invites Crouch to chair the symposium, where Archie himself will take McFee's place.

As his Secretary leaves (p. 82/81) George sees blood on her coat and realises it must have come from above his wardrobe. There he finds his hare, Thumper, impaled on the arrow he himself accidentally fired on p. 13/28. As he steps wretchedly down he treads on his tortoise and kills that too. The act ends in his sobs.

The Coda (tailpiece) is the symposium, in '*bizarre dream form*'. Archie's unintelligible speech is awarded scores as if in a gymnastic contest. Then he calls witnesses as if in a court: an astronaut to testify to mankind's 'natural' selfishness; Tarzan of the Apes to show that moral values are 'merely the products of civilisation'; and the new Archbishop of Canterbury – who, to Archie's dismay, then turns into a contrary witness, having warmed to his new job, and is briskly shot. Archie's final witness is Dotty, who sings a song of philosophical relativism, where two and two makes only 'roughly' four. George shouts for silence (p. 89/86) and gives us part of his lecture, claiming that even relativists are intuitionists at heart. But Archie caps this with a speech of total cynicism. The play ends with a sad one-line solo from Dotty, still mourning the violation of the moon.

Philosophy

The satire in this play extends to philosophy itself, the intellectual field which is most often associated with Stoppard, but on which his attitude is, as on many other topics, ambivalent. The philosophical questions he writes about are 'in fact the kind of propositions that would occur to any intelligent person in his bath' or 'are battled about in most bars on most nights' (*In Conversation; Gussow*). When philosophy becomes academic, it can seem 'absurd ... the entire operation seems to be taking place in a large plastic bubble' – though, on the other hand, 'I enjoyed the rules that philosophers play by' (*Sunday Times*, 1974). Many non-philosophers will recognise this feeling that the subject is an artificial game. For the sake of clarity, philosophers tend to use simplified imaginary examples which deliberately risk silliness. With his hare and tortoise and bow and arrow, George looks like a child (or madman) at play; and Archie's Jumpers are a physical caricature of dubious mental gymnastics. *Jumpers* is a serious study of men disagreeing about matters of fundamental importance, but at the same time a cartoon mocking their antics.

Philosophy attempts to make sense of our existence by the skills of reasoning. Philosophers generally expect each other to produce logical defences for their views rather than merely assert their religious faith or intuition, but there have been intuitionist philosophers prepared to insist on their gut feelings, and Stoppard's George is one.

The progress of philosophy over the centuries can seem in some ways the very opposite of progress: the steady demolition of previous assumptions. By the early twentieth century, philosophy was much involved with problems in mathematics (as in the work of Bertrand Russell); later its emphasis shifted to questioning the actual language we use – as in the work of Ludwig Wittgenstein, whose name George borrows for a phone call. In the 1920s and 1930s Logical Positivism, best known in Britain through the work of A. J. Ayer, attempted to demolish much of philosophy itself, claiming that it should be restricted to matters which were scientifically verifiable (as roughly in Dotty's version of Archie, p. 29/41). Slightly later, Behaviourists such as B. F. Skinner – Stoppard once described *Jumpers* as an 'anti-Skinner play' – claimed that apparent free will was merely a matter of conditioned responses, like those trained into dogs. George wants to turn the clock back forty years from all this uncertainty: he feels it has been bad for our moral thinking. (To some extent he is echoing a real British philosopher, C. E. M. Joad, who suggested in 1950 that Logical Positivism could lead to undesirable effects.) The cleverer and more educated people are, the more they seem tempted to jump about like gymnasts and never take up a firm moral position.

Reasonably enough, *Jumpers* never tries to offer new thinking itself. 'The play,' said Jonathan Bennett to fellow philosophers in 1975, 'has a musty, out-of-date quality, as though for Stoppard philosophy had died in about 1935.' But that is George's declared intention: 'I had hoped to set British moral philosophy back forty years' (p. 35/46). And to the average audience in 1972, as distinct from professional philosophers, the discussion may not have seemed so very out of date.

Stoppard may have been pushing his luck, however, when he claimed to *Theatre Quarterly* that in this play he had made 'coherent a fairly complicated intellectual argument'. Its coherence isn't always obvious in the theatre, and though George can drop the names of philosophers and mathematicians, the ideas through which he stumbles don't go all that far beyond what might 'occur to any intelligent person in his bath'. Indeed if they did, they might kill the play. Much of George's case seems to be not argument at all, more a declaration of a leap of faith. And of course Stoppard at the same time needs him to be a comically futile figure – a man whose very job is thinking is seen getting pathetically muddled: it's a bit like seeing a former Tour de France cyclist almost unable to stay on his bike.

Thus, *Jumpers* is no more seriously offered as a critique of modern philosophy than *Rosencrantz* is of Shakespeare's *Hamlet*. Stoppard is writing plays, not specialist disquisitions; but he does like to sketch in an intellectual *background* which interests him. In *Jumpers* we are shown a man who believes in 'right and wrong', and indeed in God, surrounded by smoother-talking intellectuals who have rejected those beliefs. They, and the government they have helped to elect, are prepared to bend any moral principle to suit their convenience. And the erosion of certainties has reached the heart of George's personal life: his wife is in a state of breakdown, which he seems unable to help, and she may (or of course may not) be having an affair with the smoothest talker of all.

An uneasy complication is Stoppard's decision to give George and his wife the names of a previous real-life professor of moral philosophy, G. E. Moore, and his wife Dorothy. Moore had some reputation for being ineffectual in everyday matters, as George is, and may, as George claims (p. 63/67), have insisted on the 'right to recognise [goodness] when he saw it'; yet, as George also says, he was a humanist, and arguably his *Principia Ethica* paved the way for Logical Positivism. Particularly when 'Dorothy' is shortened to Dotty (slang for mentally unbalanced), the use of these real people's names seems in doubtful taste.

Page-by-page notes are given later. Here a closer look will be taken at some key passages. Sometimes (pp. 45–6/52–4) George's argument is entirely coherent; at other times we glimpse only a rough direction within his bumbling.

The existence of God

George's first problem (p. 10/24) is language itself: even using the term 'God' can seem to imply that something/body of the kind exists. He gets into an instant muddle over this and it looks as if his whole lecture may be only gibberish.

At 'Secondly', however, he becomes more coherent. In former centuries religious belief was general and atheism the exception; now (p. 11/25) the tide has turned the other way. And yet there remain two basic reasons for the idea of God: to explain Creation (how did the universe happen?) and to explain our moral feelings (which George is certain we have, but where do they come from?).

The God of Creation

On pp. 12–15/26–9 George is pursuing the first of these, the ancient question of the First Cause or (p. 14/29) the Unmoved Mover. Some mathematicians and theoreticians have denied the necessity of this 'first term', because if there is infinity upwards in number (Cantor), there can equally be ever smaller fractions, with no necessary final (or original) point. George hopes to discredit this argument by tying it to Zeno's obviously absurd theory that an arrow never gets to its target: a classic example of abstract ideas ignoring (p. 15/29) 'experience'. Arrows do reach their targets, and by actually firing one during his lecture George will claim to defeat the mathematical objection to the necessity of a First Cause.

'Good and bad' are only expressions of feelings

On p. 29/41 Dotty summarises what she has learnt from Archie. Things only 'are', or can 'be', when their attributes are verifiable by others (e.g., being green or waterproof). Assertions of value or ethics remain merely opinions or 'feelings'. If extended this means that no act, not even murder, can be definably 'bad' – let alone 'good'. Such terms (see George's hostile summary on p. 28/48–9) are 'of our own making', merely 'social conventions': he believes that this view is the 'orthodox mainstream' against him.

'The irreducible fact of goodness'

On such mainstream lines George's opponent McFee (pp. 45–6/53–4) has claimed that moral judgement ('good man') is of the same kind as aesthetic judgement ('good music'), meaning 'different things to different people at different times'. George dismisses this as 'an exercise which combines simplicity with futility', because no one would disagree with it and it tells us nothing useful (p. 46/54). It is merely a comment on the *language* we use, not on our real *values*.

George then turns his opponent's material against him. McFee has also shown that different cultures 'honour' their elders in different and apparently contradictory ways; but George implies that it is naïve not to *expect* such differences. The remarkable thing is the sameness of intention – the idea of honouring elders at all – recurring in two widely different cultures. To crow over the fact that different codes of good conduct exist is to highlight, yet signally fail to explore, the impulse to behave well. What is significant is that every society has some concepts, and indeed instincts, of goodness, honour and relative value. Where do these concepts or instincts themselves come from? (George's implied answer – from God – remains unstated here.)

Pages 61–3/66–7 revise the last two points. The word 'good' cannot be reduced just to an opinion about a bacon sandwich. What is the motive for kindness, if not God? (though even George feels this may 'push my convictions to absurdity'). Archie's speech (p. 64/68) is delicately balanced ('careful phrasing') between a token respect for George's view ('Even if there is') and a liberal humanism ('Man is the highest form ... duties and rights ... choosing seems to be a genuine human possibility').

The limiting curve

Professionally, George has hit rock bottom at the start of his long speech on p. 68/71. 'How the hell does one know what to believe?' is the sort of question philosophers are supposed to help us *answer*, as is 'how do we know that we *know* anything?' His basic bewilderment is at least honest (and happens to chime with Stoppard's own statements at the time) but is confused and confusing, particularly when he brings in God. After saying that he doesn't 'claim to know', George is a moment later doing just that: 'I tell you I *know*.' This may be emotionally stirring but has no philosophical value (because it remains merely assertion, not argument). George himself feels its weakness: 'I sound like a joke vicar.'

The image of the limiting curve (p. 69) is more rational: a perfect circle must exist in infinity, because it is 'logically implied by the existence of polygons'. (This seems essentially the same argument George used earlier, contradicting Cantor: ultimately the series of fractions must end, the straight-lined sides must blend into a perfect circle somewhere, because arrows do reach their targets. George is arguing from 'experience' – of arrows – back into theory.) But by the bottom of p. 69/72 this in turn has reverted to an emotional expression of religious faith: the fact that we live and can question our existence suggests some perfection beyond. This is 'mysticism', not argument; and George instantly feels it is 'of staggering banality' (obviousness and unoriginality; see, for example, Robert Browning's popular poem 'Abt Vogler' of 1864: 'On the earth, the broken arcs; in the heaven, the perfect round').

Everyone is intuitionist really

In his final speech (p. 89/87) George claims that even relativists have gut feelings about basic values (life over death, love over hate) and fail to see this as inconsistency. It is a final appeal to common sense, or an instinct of goodness; in later writing Stoppard will refer to 'natural justice', as instinctively felt by a child not yet 'corrupted' by cleverness.

Characters and Cartoons

Dotty's problem with the moon is shared by Penelope in the television play out of which *Jumpers* grew: *Another*

Moon Called Earth, shown by the BBC in June 1967. That was two years before anyone actually set foot on the moon, but in the TV play a 'lunanaut' has just done so, and has returned to earth for a ceremonial parade which is now in progress. Penelope wants to see his face:

> to see if it shows, what he has seen ... He has stood outside and seen us whole, all in one go, little. And suddenly everything we live by – our rules – our good, our evil – our ideas of love, duty – all the things we've counted on as absolute truths – because we filled all existence – they're all suddenly exposed as nothing more than local customs – nothing more – because he has seen the edges where we stop ... when that thought drips through to the bottom, people won't just carry on. The things they've taken on trust, they've never had edges before.

We live on 'just another moon called Earth'. The lunanaut has 'made it all random'. This is the exact opposite of what Penelope's husband, Bone (the young Stoppard disconcertingly shifted names about) is trying to prove: he is a historian attempting to show that nothing ever happens at random: there is a fixed logic to everything.

The lines quoted above are clearly the origin of Dotty's speech on p. 73/75, and a simplified guide to it. In *Jumpers*, Dotty's problem has to yield centre stage to other material, and is also expressed in more elaborate language. The doctor, Albert, who visits Penelope in bed, has developed into the more substantial and sinister figure of Archie, as George is a more substantial and sympathetic replacement for Bone. A cartoon idea, the

opposition of two absurdly extreme views (either everything or nothing is random), has been transformed into a
much more complex debate – taking place, moreover, at a
time when the whole nation is to be governed according
to relativist views.

Yet the presentation remains in cartoon mode. Bones is
a Monty Python policeman and Crouch ('it's as much as
my job's worth') an entirely predictable caretaker – until
he proves, with cartoon *un*predictability, knowledgeable
about philosophy. Archie, Stoppard's only real villain, is
entirely a fantasy figure (doctor of almost everything, and
coroner as well as Vice-Chancellor): yet far from being
out of place in this play he might be said to command its
idiom (see below, this book, p. 82) and preside over its
action, introducing it and organising the ending of both
acts. Dotty's malady remains as absurd as Penelope's, and
George's intention to use a hare and a tortoise in his
lecture is not only bizarre but also based on a quite
elementary confusion, between a paradox of Zeno and a
fable of Aesop.

The play's most hilarious cartoon moment is also its
most painful – George, holding the bloody corpse of
Thumper, stepping fatally on Pat. On the final page he
speaks of Thumper as 'my late friend', and we may
wonder how many other friends he has had. When he
earlier (p. 17/31) uses the same words about Bertrand
Russell, Dotty insists that 'he wasn't your friend ... He
was *my* friend' (a side-glance at Russell's reputation as an
amorous type). We should understand that George is as
disabled as Dotty, in different ways. When he speaks, on
the same page, of trying to get Russell 'away from the
day-to-day parochialism of international politics' it is a
funny line, but it seems he may actually mean it, and

Dotty is more or less right to retort that he is 'living in dreamland' whereas she, since the moon landings, is 'without a dream in my heart'. Busy in his abstract pursuit of goodness, George has actually ceased to do good. Dotty was at least superb at her work (we see her 'gowned, coiffed, stunning' on p. 44/52 and hear her record – which should sound wonderful – on pp. 47–8/55–6), but George knows that 'I cut a ludicrous figure in the academic world' and admits that 'I can't seem to find the words.' And he fails her in what seems his only significant human relationship.

By the end of Act One, audiences may have warmed to George's argument (which has temporarily lost its incoherence) and by the end of the play they may pity him; but his early behaviour seems first ridiculous (calling the police to complain about noise in his own apartment) and then monstrously insensitive. When a wife successively calls 'Help!' 'Murder!' 'Horror!' and 'Rape!', her husband does owe *some* kind of attention. When George at last responds he sounds not even like her former tutor but more like a crabbed schoolmaster – 'I will not have ... delinquency!' (p. 12/26), 'Will you stop this childish nonsense!' – and his objections are entirely selfish, to do with his own ('dreamland') work: he never, for example, suggests that Dotty's antics may be unhelpful for *her*.

They are still cartoon characters in a cartoon world (they might perhaps be found in some TV sitcoms, but definitely not in a realist soap), but the stylisation of a cartoon, as the political pages of newspapers show, can sharply indicate truth. Stoppard clearly intended his play to be balanced: A and minus A (see this book, p. 17). Dotty has developed a distorted perspective, and is entranced by a satanic spirit (Archie), but nevertheless she remains sensual, warm, in some ways loving, and definitely in need. George has better instincts about what should guide our lives, but is making a thorough mess of guiding his own, or anyone else's. Stoppard's own comment is:

> it tried to be a moral play, because while George has the right ideas, he is also a culpable person; while he is defending his ideas and attacking the opposition, he is also neglecting everyone around him and shutting out his wife who is in need, not to mention shooting his hare and stepping on his tortoise. (*In Conversation; Guppy*).

To blame George for the deaths of Thumper and Pat may seem harsh; but what is being disclosed here is a dramatist's own mental balance-sheet. Perhaps George *deserved* to lose his animal friends.

This division of sympathy was strongly reinforced in the original (1972) Coda. When Archbishop Clegthorpe started protesting on behalf of his flock (p. 87/85), Archie's line was that of Henry II: 'Will no one rid me of this turbulent priest?' (the 1984 'copper's nark' is much cruder). Jumpers then leapt either side of Clegthorpe, with music 'to choreograph the threat'. In a rapid series of gymnastic movements he was moved upstage to form part of a pyramid of Jumpers – within which, of course, McFee was shot in the opening scene. George began a nervous protest: 'Point of order, Mr Chairman', and Clegthorpe appealed directly to him: 'Professor – it's not right. George – help.' But then George failed him, apparently intimidated: 'Er ... this seems to be a political quarrel', whereupon Clegthorpe was shot.

For the following dozen years this moment was seen as crucial by commentators (including me). At the end of the play, when sympathy for George might well be at its height, it showed him being strikingly 'culpable', losing his moral nerve. The far shorter 1984 version ('definitive', we are told) significantly shifts the balance, no longer challenging George to show his colours (Clegthorpe's dying cry of his name merely baffles an audience unfamiliar with the original). George's own cry of 'Dotty!' is an addition, seeming to suggest that he believes her to have fired both shots (McFee's and Clegthorpe's). Thus Archie has been made that much coarser ('copper's nark') and George virtually blameless, and Dotty has been half re-accused. In this case, we may wonder if the passing of years – perhaps a firming-up of Stoppard's own beliefs? – have caused him to turn down the volume of his 'minus A'. If so, I have tended to regret the change.

And yet (my own 'minus A') it could be that the dramatist eventually felt that the forces of Archie already dominate quite enough. This idea may become clearer as we consider the play's staging.

Stagecraft

Archie's play

Jumpers begins in a mode it doesn't develop, that of a spectacular revue (a show mixing song, dance and sketches). I can remember, before seeing the play, hearing it 'hyped' and feeling enormously excited at the prospect of a theatre piece which might somehow bring together philosophy and acrobatics. I vaguely imagined something like Peter Brook's celebrated production of *A Midsummer*

Night's Dream, which had used flying trapezes. With such expectations, I was bound to feel some disappointment at a play where the Jumpers are 'not especially talented' and where they are used so little. I felt (and still do) like the critic who saw *Rosencrantz* as wasting a 'noble conception' (see this book, p. 233).

But Stoppard had other intentions. Each element of the spectacular revue almost instantly crashes. Dotty's humiliation, in the very first moments, embarrasses the audience; as with the 'death' of the Player (see p. 43 in this book) there's a remote possibility that it's real. The complex stage-business with swing, Secretary and Crouch is skilled and highly entertaining – but then ends in a crash of broken glass. And the Jumpers' pyramid forms itself to hopelessly confused music, and is suddenly horribly holed by a gunshot.

In this revue everything has gone about as wrong as it could, introducing a world where, for everyone except the likes of Archie, things in general have also gone wrong. Visually it is sinister that the Jumpers' pyramid maintains itself 'intact ... defying gravity' in the silence while Dotty walks through the gap, and the dying McFee drags himself bloodily up against her. It seems an emblem of indifference. A few moments later Archie is telling Dotty 'there's no need to get it out of proportion', and we move into the hideous joke of Scott knocking Oates to the ground. At 'I may be gone for some time', an audience is likely to howl with laughter; but that laughter partly involves us in Scott's callousness.

As we go home after *Jumpers*, what we recall most may be George's voice, and his pleas for our moral instinct. If so, that is surely what Stoppard intended. Yet almost everything in the structure and discourse of this play points the opposite way; as a piece of theatre it is flashy, sharp, brilliant and relatively harsh – far more likely to have been written by Archie than by George. And Archie is its ringmaster, its master of ceremonies (pp. 1 and 90/18 and 87). Earlier I called this play a satire, and a good satire does not relent.

The three areas

Students unable to see a performance of *Jumpers* should make a particular effort to visualise the 'three playing areas' (p. vii/13). Those with computer 'drawing' facilities can sketch a plan (from overhead) and then trace the action as it shifts about. The theatre audience may not overtly note any of this, but in an effective production will subconsciously absorb the significance of the three areas. This is a complex play, ingeniously scored for the stage. The first scene and the Coda are performed in undefined space: spotlights for the party, stained-glass projections for the Coda. But for all the rest:

The study is George's realm, where he pursues his ideas and gives commands to his Secretary (though she never speaks and finally shows that she has preserved complete independence). The bedroom is Dotty's space, where she is trapped except in the first scene and Coda; and the hall is the region of Bones, the common man investigating wrong-doing, who is also the stage-door worshipper. Each is the dominant figure in his or her own area, usually saying most and scoring most laughs; for example, although on p. 38/48 George uneasily expounds philosophy in the hall, he does so reluctantly, under Bones's sceptical pressure; and although on p. 59/63 Archie attempts to corrupt Bones in the hall, he fails – it's when

Bones is caught on Dotty's territory (p. 68/71) that he is done for.

Archie does not have an 'area'; he has access to them all, moving snake-like everywhere, untroubled by scruple. On p. 63/67 he 'quietly lets himself into the study'. We are more or less used to him strolling into Dotty's bedroom: he is after all her psychiatrist and may also be having an affair with her. But it is altogether more disturbing to see him encroach on George's domain, and even appear to *let himself in*, as if he somehow controls all locks and keys.

This dark play shows Dotty's alienation and Archie's cyncicism steadily making inroads upon George's efforts to assert the existence of goodness. Dotty's cry of 'Fire!' from her area (p. 13/28) causes George to fire the arrow that kills Thumper: the cry from the bedroom destroys the innocence in the study ('Herr Thumper, who was innocent as a rainbow'). By p. 78/79, even an elderly caretaker has taken over George's space and is chuckling at the inadequacy of his professional argument. On pp. 79–80/79–80, though in his own domain, George has become tongue-tied, still struggling with Crouch's instant criticism of his script; the person moving in the study is not George but his Secretary, suddenly a figure of significance – while Archie and Crouch converse about McFee in the hall. Now George looks disabled and marginalised even within his own space. When he is at last left alone, and *investigates* that space, he discovers one 'friend', one example to support his proposed argument, dead; and then steps backwards to kill the other.

Textual Notes

Act One

vii/13   *Film and slides* ... – such back-projections are associated with the left-wing theatre of Bertolt Brecht (1898–1956). Their use here therefore carries some irony, since Stoppard might see his Rad-Libs (who turn a vet into an archbishop) as the natural outcome of Brecht's political reasoning.

ix/14   is a dandy – a crucial indicator. See discussion above, this book, pp. 17–18.

1/17   *dries* – forgets her part.

    2   pseudonymous – under a false name. We gather that the answer George gets, reasonably enough, is No; but he proceeds to give a false name anyway, that of Ludwig Wittgenstein (1889–1951), Austrian philosopher of language. id – a term from psychology: the instinctual, unconscious part of the mind.

2/18   INCREDIBLE – Dotty's subsequent complaints about the misuse of this word suggest her philosophical training.

  – RADICAL – the word, taken seriously by George on p. 27, means being prepared to go back to the roots of accepted ideas and question them fundamentally.

  – LIBERAL – suggests a more relaxed, tolerant approach. The Rad-Libs are permissive at a 'radical' level, even about basic moral questions.

4/19   the one about the moon – but of course there

are many such songs, and Dotty proceeds to muddle several of them.

5/20 *chanteuse* – female night-club singer.

6 There's no need ... – we hear Archie's drawling indifference before we hear George's assertion of traditional values; and similarly it is Archie who will end the play. The Archie-voice is always urbane, never confrontational.
a great pity of course – are the words of a civilised old-fashioned English gent, with a hint of stiff-upper-lip.
it's not as though ... – Archie's idea seems to be that if we die for ever, it doesn't much matter when.

8/23 Captain Scott ... some time – A 'sick-humour' reversal of a famous self-sacrifice. In 1912 Captain Robert Scott's team were the first English expedition to reach the South Pole (as this team is the first to reach the moon), but all died on the return journey. Captain Lawrence Oates, realising his frostbitten feet were holding back his companions, walked out into a blizzard to die, saying simply, 'I am just going out and may be some time.'

9/24 Oh, horror ... murder! – comes from the point in Shakespeare's *Macbeth* at which a murder victim is discovered, having lain in the house all night. Traditionally it is unlucky to quote *Macbeth* in a theatre. 'Woe ... house?' is the notoriously weak response of the guilty hostess, Lady Macbeth.

– To begin ... – George's philosophy lecture is not nonsense, and at times seems to represent

Stoppard's own views; but his thoughts and his language repeatedly chase their own tails – as at the bottom of this page, where the word 'late' (Russell had died just two years before *Jumpers* was first performed) keeps misplacing itself. A distant source seems to be Lucky's speech in Beckett's *Waiting for Godot*, where a philosophical thread of argument is seen in a far more advanced state of decomposition.

– Russell – Bertrand Russell – (1872–1970) was a hereditary earl, mathematician and philosopher. He published (with A. N. Whitehead) his *Principia Mathematica* in 1913. He was a contemporary and friend of G. E. Moore.

– necrophiliac – sexually attracted to the dead.

10/24 predicates – here, attributes. Russell's *Theory of Descriptions* was a way round the absurdity of 'Is God?' He argued that to talk of something existing is to *describe* it, and that 'God' is not a proper name but a descriptive term summing up a number of predicates which may or may not include existence. 'Is God?' is not questioning a predicate which is certain.

– omniscience – knowing everything.

– Plato – Greek philosopher (427–347 BC).

11/25 onus – burden, responsibility.

– the noes had it – the result of a debate where the opposition has won.

– Professor Ramsey – F. P. Ramsey (1903–30) died too young to be a professor, but worked at Cambridge along lines opened by Russell and Wittgenstein. He rejected the idea of truths beyond the limits of language. 'Theology' studies religion; 'ethics' studies morals.

- the chance product of universal gases – a non-religious, scientific explanation of the origin of the universe.

- Quite – Dolly's cry coincidentally sums up George's 'Is/Are God?'

12/26 Wolf – to cry wolf is to raise a false alarm (in legend, a boy who repeatedly did so was eventually faced by a real wolf, but his cries were ignored).

- lupine – wolf-like. Did George mean to say 'lunatic'?

12/27 hardy perennial – question which (like some plants) comes back year after year.

- overly engaging – too informal (he means the bow and arrow).

- *raison d'être* – reason (justification) for existence. The First Cause argument says that God is a philosophical necessity, which logic demands.

13/27 soubriquet – nickname.

- My old friend – he prevents himself from mentioning Russell again.

- series of proper fractions – strictly this is not a series; but George is right in saying that it has no smallest or greatest member.

- the Greek philosopher – ancient Greeks proved that there is no greatest (or smallest) number. Georg Cantor (1845–1918) studied the concept of infinity.

- Zeno – of Elea, Greek philosopher (490–430 BC)

- *ad infinitum* – for ever.

13/28 as I will now demonstrate – George will
actually show the opposite, proving Zeno's
paradox absurd (see middle of p. 15/29).

– Saint Sebastian – was sentenced to die by being
shot with arrows.

14/28 contingent – happening by chance not necessity.

– Aristotle – Greek philosopher (384–322 BC)
taught that all matter is potentially alive and
striving to attain its particular form. There is a
whole series from the simplest kind of matter to
the perfect living individual, behind which there
must be a supreme source: the Unmoved
Mover.

– at the mouth of our cave – a reference to Plato's
allegory of the cave. At the mouth of the cave is
the fire; man sits in the cave with his back to it,
perceiving reality only through the flickering
shadows cast on the cave wall.

14/29 St Thomas Aquinas – philosopher and
theologian (1225–74) who developed Aristotle's
Unmoved Mover into a Christian divinity.

15/29 the point of a converging series – according to
mathematicians, an infinite series (for example,
the fractions of distance before the arrow
reaches its target) can still have a finite sum
(the total distance between the bow and the
target).

– fallacy – logical error.

– paradoxes – are apparent self-contradictions.

– tortoise ... hare – Zeno's paradox is about
Achilles, the legendary athlete, and a tortoise.
George has muddled this with Aesop's fable in

which a tortoise wins its race against a hare by steady, slow persistence.

16/30 *The Naked and the Dead* – novel by (1948) Norman Mailer.

– let you – i.e., allow him sex; see also p. 18/31, 'insult' and p. 19 'ration book'.

17/31 metaphysical – here, unreal, belonging to philosophical theory.

– John Peel – huntsman famed in song.

– Mao Tse Tung – the Communist ruler of China from 1949 to 1976, he was famously telephoned in the cause of world peace by the elderly Russell.

– parochialism – narrowness, confined to local affairs.

18/31 *contrition* – repentance of wrongdoing.

18/32 salon – under this term, eighteenth-century French aristocrats were accustomed to 'receive' respectful visitors while in bed.

– panache – elegant style; just what George lacks and Archie has. Actually, what Dotty wants is much more than mere style, it is assistance in corrupting the course of justice by concealing a murder. That she should confuse the two, even calling the latter 'rising *above*', is ominous.

19/32 ration book – i.e., for a fixed weekly or monthly allowance.

20/33 hyacinth girl ... growing thin – quotations from two poems by T. S. Eliot: *The Waste Land* and 'The Love Song of J. Alfred Prufrock', where the speakers are nervous male lovers.

– fell among theatricals – the Good Samaritan

(see note to p. 57) helped someone who 'fell among thieves' (Luke 10: 30).

21/34 *coup d'état* – unelected seizure of state power.

22/34 skeletons ... wash – Stoppard repeatedly mocks the mixing of clichés.

– And yet, Professor – the student who hoped to sit quiet and not be thought stupid in George's class (p. 20/33) evidently learned a lot. Dotty can speak as fluently as anyone.

23/35 Ryle ... Ayer – Gilbert Ryle (1906–76) and A. J. Ayer (see note to p. 29/41) were British philosophers.

– knowledge – in English we have the one word 'knowledge' (where French, for example, has at least two) with several different meanings. In 'the biblical sense' 'he knew her' means he had sex with her.

24/36 I mean ... – here George becomes sarcastic.

– 'The Moon and Sixpence' – the title of a novel (1919) by W. Somerset Maugham.

25/37 The Thirty-Nine Articles – principles of Anglican doctrine.

– rationalised – logically restructured. But in industry the word heralds job losses; so George's 'You can't rationalise' is ambiguous. Firstly, he takes it for granted that the Thirty-Nine Articles are fundamentally irrational, matters of faith not logic; secondly, he is appalled at the reductions which are likely to follow.

26/38 uncoped ... Dis-mantled ... mitre – a cope is an archbishop's mantle, and the mitre is his headdress.

- belted raincoats – as worn, say, by movie
  detectives or secret agents.
- Lucifer – in Judaeo-Christian mythology the
  top angel, who rebelled against God and was
  sent falling through space to hell. Though the
  line comes from Dotty, it is George who might
  see the Rad-Libs as rebelling like Lucifer.
- When they first landed – i.e., on the moon. This
  caused Dotty to go to pieces, feeling that once
  such an 'impossibility' had proved possible,
  why should there not be unicorns? In
  Stoppard's *Rosencrantz* it is suggested that a
  unicorn seen repeatedly would become
  'common experience'.

27/39 Freudian – a psychoanalyst follower of
  Sigmund Freud, inclined to seek sexual
  significances (e.g., unicorn's horn = penis).
- scientism – faith that materialist science can
  answer all questions.
- gone ape – slang for 'started to behave like a
  beast', therefore a reversal of Charles Darwin
  (1809–82)'s discovery that humans developed
  from apes.

28/40 premises – (in philosophy) basic propositions.
- soya beans – presumably because they give
  efficient, if not very tasty, nutrition. George
  decides to see as 'irrational' (some might prefer
  to say 'non-utilitarian') anything that is not
  strictly functional – in other words most of the
  things we enjoy.
- The irrational ... absolutes – Reason is a
  'civilising force' because there is so much
  natural irrationality in people. But in a world

91

where everyone behaved and thought rationally the 'moralist' would seem like a crank, claiming non-rational certitude. This difficult speech introduces George's intuitionist dilemma: as a philosopher he believes in reason, but he has moral instincts and intuitions which seem to come from somewhere outside his reasoning faculty.

– Doings ... Thingummy – common substitutes when a name can't be remembered.

29/41 plastic bag – much used by the cleaning lady; but it sets Dotty thinking ahead to p. 48/56.

– There's no question ... – this speech, which represents Archie's thinking and also the logical positivism of A. J. Ayer (1910–89) and others, is clarified in its final sentence . 'Green or square', etc., are seen as factual attributes; 'good ... bad', etc., as merely 'expressions of our feelings'.

knows not 'seems' – a quotation from Shakespeare's *Hamlet*.

– I don't feel so good – these simple words are weighted by echoes of the previous lines. The speech goes on with references to the moon in songs and poems, from days when '*things were in place*' (i.e., for Dotty, before the first moon landing).

30 D'ye ken ... – in the folk-song it is John Peel (see p. 17) who has a 'coat so gay'.

31/42 *a priori* – (philosophical term) self-evident or presumed: something we have always known. George here seems to be resorting to mere assertion – which is perhaps why he imagines his audience calling for him to 'Resign'.

32/43 *Lulu's* back! – in town – a popular song.

– Now might I ... – the tortoise's name provides this pun. George turns down the chance to fire an arrow into Archie (who he believes is the other side of the door). Shakespeare's Hamlet turns down an unexpected chance to kill his stepfather Claudius, and whispers to himself, 'Now might I do it pat' (where 'pat' means swiftly or neatly). Hamlet and George could hardly be more different, except that thinking hinders both of them from acting. We have just seen (p. 30) George abandoning his desperate wife in order to get back to drafting his lecture.

– The door is opened to him ... – Stoppard's early plays delight in contriving natural explanations for absurd combinations of circumstance. *After Magritte* (1970, two years before *Jumpers*) turns on a series of such explanations, the true one also involving a face covered with shaving foam.

32/44 dem bones ... dry bones – comes from another once-popular song.

33/44 No really? – George's appearance certainly suggests he might need a psychiatrist.

– I'm very glad ... – cliché cop's line, implying 'you've given yourself away'.

– helping me in my inquiries – a British police euphemism for 'being interrogated'.

– *lightening* – joking because Bones's elementary working-out of who George is seemed (see '*shrewdly*') like some major logical deduction.

34/45 Charlie – Bones proceeds to call George by many different names (some satire on police indifference?)

35/46 symposium – academic discussion with prepared contributions.

36/47 I'm your man – George assumes (being unaware of the dead body, and because Bones referred to a phone call) that Bones is simply here to investigate George's own complaint (p. 2). This is traditional comic misunderstanding, particularly acute on pp. 41/49 (with Dotty) and 53/59 (with Bones). It is not until p. 76/78 that George finds out the truth.

37/47 a side of her – a faint pun (the Secretary was naked on the chandelier).

38/48 riposte – reply.

– approved of – compare Dotty's speech, pp. 31–2.

40/49 The difference is ... a line that Stoppard himself has used in conversation.

42/50 Logical positivists ... – all the acrobats reject George's beliefs in fundamental moral truths. Logical positivists taught that the only meaningful statements are those which can be validated by sense-experience. Jeremy Bentham (1748–1832) believed that society should be run not according to traditional religious or moral principles, but according to 'utility': promoting 'the greatest happiness for the greatest number'. Immanuel Kant (1724–1804) was the pioneer of much modern rationalist thinking. Empiricists teach that all concepts are derived from experience; all statements claiming to express knowledge depend on experience for their justification. Behaviourists explain all behaviour in terms of conditioned responses.

- first-rate gymnast ... indifferent philosopher – see note to p. 44/51.

- Chair – professorship.

- below the salt – lower in esteem (originally, placed further from the host at a grand dinner).

43/51 the Athens – i.e., the top city for philosophy.

44/52 *coiffed* – with her hair done up elegantly.

Fidelio – opera by Beethoven, where the trumpet promises liberation.

- Professor McFee ... – from here to its end on p. 47/55 George's speech is no longer confused. He advances a coherent argument, particularly on pp. 46–7/54–5, where perhaps we hear something like Stoppard's own voice.

- bends over backwards ... jumping through the Vice-Chancellor's hoop – the central image of *Jumpers* becomes clear. In George's (and perhaps Stoppard's) view these thinkers are absurdly 'acrobatic' in their thinking, arranging themselves in ingenious but unlikely 'positions'.

- aesthetic – to do with beauty or artistic taste; so (in McFee's opinion) subjective, not absolute.

45 *Tarzan of the Apes* – popular novel (1914) by Edgar Rice Burroughs; the plot is outlined on p. 85.

mysterious property of the music – George clearly has an intuitionist faith in absolute values in art as well as in morality.

46/54 *reductio ad absurdum* – in philosophy, a

demonstration that an argument is false by taking it to its logical extreme.

– deeply-rutted garden path – to lead up a garden path is to mislead; 'deeply-rutted' – far too many people have wandered here before.

47/55 altruistic – benevolent, without self-interest.

– Hobbes – Thomas Hobbes (1588–1679), author of *Leviathan*, was an English materialist who might well have given the answer imagined here.

Act Two

50/57 G. E. Moore – (1873–1958), a close friend of Bertrand Russell, published *Principia Ethica* in 1903. See also this book, p. 71.

51/58 *Language, Truth and God* – an imaginary riposte to A. J. Ayer's best-known book, *Language, Truth and Logic*.

– consummate – complete, perfect. This makes George think of sexual consummation, which Dotty is denying him; but Bones still has in mind her retirement from singing; thus their next two lines are at cross-purposes.

– osteopath – one who treats conditions of the bones.

52/58 psychiatric expert witness – as Dotty's fan, Bones is already planning how to get her off a murder charge.

53/59 are all the same – Bones thinks George is talking about murder, and thus links him to the non-moralist thinkers George is actually against.

  – to go easy on you – because, on p. 41/50,
   George told her he would 'take the blame'.

55/61 What happened to ... – Archie still takes Bones
   to be some kind of servant replacing the
   cleaning lady.

  – Cognomen – nickname or appropriate name;
   'syndrome' medical condition.

56/62 a vacancy – i.e., after McFee's death.

57/63 Sigmund – Sigmund Freud (see note to p. 27/
   39) was a psychiatrist like Archie.

58/64 an ice-pick – was used to murder Leon Trotsky
   (1879–1940), who had urged the Communist
   rulers of the Soviet Union to 'return to the true
   path'.

62/66 Bedser – English cricketer, in his prime about
   twenty years before *Jumpers*. As one who
   assumes that male English traditions are at the
   centre of the world, George is shocked that the
   Secretary has never heard of him.

  – the Good Samaritan – see above, note to p. 20/
   33, spent his own time and money saving a
   mugged man, though he came from a hostile
   tribe.

62/62 step on it ... crunch – see what happens on
   p. 82/81.

63/67 humanism – atheism which still believes in
   moral values.

  – limbo – an undefined, loose state; a religious
   no-man's-land.

  – St Francis – of Assisi (1182–1226), patron saint
   of animals.

64/68 historically notorious – i.e., huge numbers of

people have been killed in the name of various gods. See also Archie's next speech.

65/68 a furious row last night – whodunnit plays traditionally offer alternative suspects. Archie follows with a 'trivial' explanation, but the row might well have been 'furious' since (see p. 80/81) McFee had changed his views entirely, and was quitting the Jumpers to become a monk.

65/69 Reykjavik – capital of Iceland (see 'Athens of the North' on p. 43/51).

66/69 a chance to prepare mine – Archie reckons he can produce as good a result in two minutes as George in weeks.

   – caretaker – a common term for a temporary stand-in. At this point only Stoppard knows that the stand-in will in fact be the professional caretaker (porter/janitor) Crouch.

   – If only to make sure – actually, if McFee were to be there 'in spirit' it would *destroy* the materialistic argument (that there is no spirit and no life after death).

66/70 open up – in this context carries a sexual innuendo, and is followed similarly in the next few speeches by 'all right in bed', 'a bit of the other' and 'keep my hand in'.

  68 Black Beauty? – a classic children's novel; *The African Queen* was a popular film.

68/71 Do not despair – St Augustine alluded to the crucifixion of a thief each side of Christ: 'Do not despair – one of the thieves was saved; do not presume – one of the thieves was damned.' Archie will blackmail Bones into not charging

Dotty (or perhaps anyone else) with McFee's death.

– How the hell ... – George's long speech on pp. 68–9/71–2 is discussed above (pp. 73–4 of this book).

so difficult to know – see this book, p. 17: 'Tom Stoppard Doesn't Know.'

69/71 postulate – propose for the sake of argument.

– *Cogito ergo deus est* – I think, so God must exist. René Descartes (1596–1650) famously stated *Cogito ergo sum* (I am thinking, so I must exist).

70/72 A vacancy – (second time) as on p. 56/62: McFee's Chair.

71/73 not seeking any favours – George thinks Archie means it is not 'ethical' to approach him at all on the subject of additional posts.

the author of *Principia Ethica* – i.e., G. E. Moore.

72 Archie – we can speculate why George (or was it Dotty?) named the goldfish after the Vice-Chancellor.

– for a charade! – see p. 24/36.

– rhetoric! – here, melodramatic language.

– *sole meunière* – a fish dish.

73/75 There is ... value – to be rationally consistent, the monk would indeed be vegetarian. But there is still (according to George) some 'rational value' in his concern for where he walks.

– egocentric – a self-centred person.

– Copernicus – Nikolaus Copernicus (1473–1543) proved that the earth goes round the sun.

– Einstein – Albert Einstein (1879–1955) found

that apparently fixed properties, such as the length of a twelve-inch ruler, actually vary according to space and time. Einstein's 'theory of relativity' is extended by thinkers such as Archie to argue that moral values are equally variable.

- to two moonmen – Dotty is thinking of p. 8/23. gnashing of unclean meats – a Biblical prophecy foresees 'weeping and wailing and gnashing of teeth' (Matthew 8: 12); the idea of teeth leads Dotty to 'meats' and thus to religious prohibitions (the Ten Commandments, Exodus 20: 1).

74/75 When did you ... – a psychiatrist's line.
- Wittgenstein – see above, note to p. 2.
- jugged – traditional way to cook hare (and George's hare is missing).

75/76 I got to know him – until late on p. 76 they remain at cross-purposes, Crouch referring to McFee, George to Thumper the hare.

77/78 what would it have *looked* like – compare the Wittgenstein story, p. 74/75.

79/79 mentor – guide or adviser.

80/80 pragmatism – a practical rather than idealistic approach: here, a polite name for amoral self-interest, which – Crouch now reveals – had begun to disgust McFee.

- twenty years hard – i.e., hard labour; when Scott gets back to earth he will be imprisoned for his selfishness. But according to McFee such conduct will be the norm in twenty years' time, under 'yellow' (i.e., Rad-Lib) rule. So great was McFee's change of heart (returning to traditional moral values) that he was about to go into a monastery – a religious commitment far greater than George's.

81/81 *Secretary snaps her handbag shut ...* – with apparent satisfaction. This is the lover whom McFee was 'terrified' to tell about his wife, and who is described on p. ix/14 as 'poker-faced, almost grim, even on her first appearance' – i.e., at the party when McFee had finally told her. She had a motive for shooting McFee, as possibly (see p.65/69) had Archie, or even (in theory) George; whereas Dotty didn't.

– dénouement – unravelling of the plot, expected at this stage in the play.

82/81 *bright splash of blood* – this may have been suggested to Stoppard by the Preface to the second edition of Ayer's *Language, Truth and Logic*, which includes the following words: 'The statement that I have blood on my coat may, in certain circumstances, confirm the hypothesis that I have committed a murder, but it is not part of the meaning of the statement that I have committed a murder that I should have blood on my coat.' Coming immediately after the snap of her handbag, the blood symbolically seems to confirm that the Secretary shot McFee. But the shot was from a distance, and in any case a moment later we learn that this blood is Thumper's. (That, however, as a logician will quickly realise, doesn't mean that she *didn't* shoot McFee.)

83/83 Coda – a tail-piece. The version now printed in the Faber edition is substantially altered from the original 1972 production: see Author's Note and also the discussion on p. 79 of this book.

- *Stained-glass* – suggests the interior of a church, but in this *'dream form'* it seems to have been converted into some unholy gymnasium.
- two minutes – observed presumably in remembrance of McFee.
- USHER: Call ... – the symposium has become a court.
- Mr Crouch ... – a few threads within Archie's *'bizarre dream'* speech: 'nucleic acids' are crucial to the fundamental chemistry of life; random tests may be a scientific method but nuclear tests were of weapons of mass destruction, and the 'testes' are the testicles, storing seeds of life. 'Universa vice' is a pun on 'vice versa'; the saying is 'necessity is the mother of invention'; 'Voltaire' (1694–1778) was a French rationalist philosopher; 'Darwin' (see above, note to p. 27/39) wrote of the origin of species; and for the last bit of nonsense see the note on Descartes on p. 69, above.

84 natural response to a pure situation – Archie implies that Scott's conduct showed human nature in essence, uninfluenced by 'culture, environment or ... history'.

- treeless Eden – i.e., without prohibitions: in the garden of Eden (Genesis) Adam and Eve were forbidden to eat from one particular tree.

85 *ululating* – making ape-like howls.

- you Tarzan – in the movie the ape-man manages to say 'I Tarzan'.

86 *one's* – aristocratic English tended to substitute

'one' for 'I'. Here the construction sounds particularly silly in a sentence beginning normally with 'I'.

– semantic – about words and meaning.

86/84 Nine – it is a score card, not the Bible oath normally read out by witnesses in court.

– For my sins – i.e., this seems to be my penance – a good-humoured mock-religious acceptance of an unpleasing obligation.

87/84 blood ... bread ... – terminology from Christian communion.

88/85 good strawberries ... send for some – adapted from Shakespeare: *Richard III*, III. iv. 31, a threatening dismissal by a future king.

– Will no one rid me – Henry II's line, requesting the assassination of another Archbishop of Canterbury, Thomas a Becket, was: 'Will no one rid me of this turbulent priest?' and these words were used in the 1972 *Jumpers*.

– copper's nark – police informer (presumably, here, too much on the side of traditional moral values).

– George! – the significant change from the original version is outlined and discussed in this book, pp. 79–80.

89/86 *Stop!!* – George claims that even Logical Positivists proceed (as he does) on common sense. They know perfectly well that Paddington does not leave the train, and also sense intuitively 'that life is better ...', etc.

89/87 east window – in a Christian church, this is behind the altar: the direction, as it were, of God.

90/87 Zeno ... – in his final words, muddling names grotesquely, George is perhaps cracking up. His pun on 'Herr' (German for Mr) is deeply groan-worthy.

– Do not despair ... saved – see above, note on p. 68. A similar allusion is made in Samuel Beckett's *Waiting for Godot*. The same play is more directly echoed in 'At the graveside' ('They give birth astride of a grave ... the gravedigger puts on the forceps'). 'Sam' was, on p. 1, the name of Dotty's piano player, but was also of course that of Beckett.

Travesties

Travesties was first performed in 1974. Though generally seen as one of Stoppard's best plays, it does present a basic difficulty: it assumes considerable advance knowledge in its audience. Whereas *Rosencrantz* may work fairly well for someone who doesn't know *Hamlet*, *Travesties* depends heavily for its laughter on prior knowledge of Oscar Wilde's comedy *The Importance of Being Earnest* (generally shortened here to *Earnest*); and ideally the spectator should also know something of *Ulysses*, the Dada movement and twentieth-century Russian history. For once, therefore, it may be better to start with background rather than with the play itself.

The first such requirement should prove enjoyable: getting to know or revising Wilde's play. It will be summarised later for revision purposes (pp. 108–10), but should first be seen (a video, perhaps) or at least read through.

The notes here start by introducing the leading figures whom Stoppard decided to bring together in *Travesties*, the point of doing so, and the reason he chose Wilde's play as a ground-base. A summary of *Earnest* is then followed by an outline of how its scheme is used by Stoppard. A critical discussion is offered, followed finally by page-by-page annotation.

The Expatriates of Zurich

Switzerland remained neutral in the First World War, and thus attracted a number of intellectuals from elsewhere in Europe. Three men living in Zurich were each ground-breaking leaders in their different fields; they did not actually know each other, but Stoppard decided to bring them together in his play. Just as he enjoys producing rational explanations of the apparently irrational, so he has often chosen to mix apparently incompatible ingredients. In this case, the three thinkers – James Joyce, Tristan Tzara and Lenin – held strong views that appear mutually exclusive: each might have disdained the beliefs of the other two. The Stoppard formula 'A minus A' could here become triple – in fact multiple, when the caricature conservative voice of Carr is added.

James Joyce

James Joyce was born in Dublin in 1882. From the age of twenty he lived largely in Continental Europe, variously in Paris, Trieste and, from 1915 to 1919, Zurich. He scraped a living by teaching, but was utterly dedicated to making himself into a great writer. He published few books, but each had been crafted with immense care over a long period. *Dubliners* (1914) has some claim to be the best book of short stories in English, and *A Portrait of the Artist as a Young Man* (1916) to be the best autobiographical novel. During the war, Joyce wrote his masterpiece, *Ulysses* (1922), a vast comic novel describing one day in Dublin – the day of Joyce's first date with his mistress and eventual wife, Nora Barnacle. His final, almost impenetrable, work was *Finnegans Wake* (1939); and he died, in Zurich once more, in 1940.

Stoppard admitted to Ronald Hayman in 1976 that

> I have a love-hate relationship with this mythical figure of the dedicated writer ... the artist who is very serious about himself and ploughs a lonely furrow and occasionally a few pages are released to the millions ... About 51 per cent of me views this figure with utter contempt and about 49 per cent with total admiration.

A and minus A, of course. Joyce seems to be in mind here, and *Travesties* gave Stoppard the chance to express both contempt and admiration, though in this case with more of the latter (see the last page of Act One: ' "I wrote *Ulysses*," he said. "What did you do?" ') Every character in the play except Lenin is a 'travesty', not an accurate biographical portrait, and Joyce's vague socialist and republican sympathies are quietly suppressed. But his case for the importance of art is eloquently voiced in the climactic speech on pp. 53–4/41–2. And the ground for that has incidentally been prepared – with marginal inconsistency – in the voice of Tzara, on p. 36/29.

Tristan Tzara

Tristan Tzara was a Romanian poet; born in 1896, he was just pushing twenty when he invented the name 'Dada' (the event is described in the play, on p. 52/40) for the new movement in art and literature founded in Zurich in 1916. Parallel rebellions took place in New York and Paris, where in 1922 an international Dada exhibition was mounted. Gradually the movement developed into Surrealism, which has lasted better – but then Tzara might well have claimed that Dada was never meant to last, nor to take on the status of traditional 'art'. The best-remembered Dadaist work is probably Marcel Duchamp's moustached 'Mona Lisa' (1919).

Dadaist thinking seems reasonably summarised in Tzara's speeches on pp. 26–8 and 40/20–3 and 41, and the history of Dada's early days in Zurich is elicited in the 'catechism' scene on pp. 49–54/38–41 (the nonsenses here are genuinely those of Dada, not invented by Stoppard). The basic idea was that the Western culture which had allowed the war to occur and was continuing to fund it must be rotten even at its supposedly sensitive core – that is, its art, which therefore should not be respected but abused. Dada similarly attacked all historical analyses (see p. 24/19, 'causality'). Though Huelsenbeck may have demanded 'radical Communism' (p. 52/41) Tzara seems to have been more an anarchist than a revolutionary. And however angry his movement claimed to be, it sounds as if it must also have been fun.

Stoppard's version of Tzara is useful in *Travesties* not only to challenge any heroic view of the war (pp. 27–8/ 22–3) but also to subvert everyone's tendency to take themselves too seriously. For this second reason, and because he at least understands the human significance of art, Tzara is the right opponent for Joyce. He also brings with him, of course, the deliberate craziness of Dada, which contributes its own laughter to the play.

Lenin

Vladimir Ilyich Ulyanov, who adopted the name of Lenin, was born in 1870 and worked as a lawyer in St Petersburg. When Lenin was seventeen his brother was executed for attempting to assassinate the Tsar; when he was twenty-five he himself was sent to Siberia for five years for spreading Marxist propaganda. He took part in the unsuccessful Russian Revolution of 1905, after which he was forced to live in exile.

In February 1917, revolution broke out again in St Petersburg (at the start of *Travesties* the news reaches Lenin). In April the Germans smuggled Lenin by train back to St Petersburg in the hope that, as indeed happened, he would gain power and withdraw Russia from the war – thus enabling Germany to concentrate on its Western Front. For Lenin to travel to Russia was therefore against Allied interests (see pp. 58–9/46 of the play). The West did eventually 'win' the war; but Lenin ruled the Soviet Union from 1917 until his death in 1924, creating a brutal totalitarian state which would wield huge international influence for most of the twentieth century. If the British Consul of the time had genuinely managed to intercept Lenin's journey, that could have altered the course of history.

Stoppard's Lenin is not at all funny, and not designed as a travesty. The reasons why he is treated so differently from the other historical figures, and the question of how well he fits into the play at all, are crucial and are discussed later (pp. 121–6).

Henry Carr

Travesties notionally takes place within the rambling memory and wishful thinking of its fourth leading male character, Henry Carr. Our edition begins (pp. ix–xii/ix–xi) with an understandably embarrassed but gracious foreword in which the dramatist outlines not only Joyce's dealings with the real Carr but facts contributed by Carr's widow after the first performance. This puts the history straight; but for the play Stoppard invented the Carr that suited him – and also Carr's fantasies, in which the name of the real Consul, Bennett, is given to his manservant. Old Cecily does point out this and other inaccuracies in the play's closing moments, pp. 90–91/70–71. Old Carr's response – and ironically this could be Tzara speaking – is 'What of it?'

The play's Carr has, like the real Carr, been invalided out of the trenches, and thus brings to the stage brief glimpses of the carnage gripping most of Europe. Also, as a conventional public-school-educated Englishman of the period, he can give voice – just as confidently as Joyce and Tzara to their opinions – to conventional middle-class male views of patriotism and art. He sees himself as the sane average man surrounded by near-lunatics; but as a chorus – a link between the action and the audience – he is distinctly untrustworthy in his weakening faculties and his keenness to present the best image of himself rather than to tell the truth. His most distinctive character trait is lifted deftly by Stoppard from a historical hint: if the real Carr spent so much on his stage costume, he could be developed as a man obsessed with his attire, so that not only the events of Earnest (pp. 42–3/34) but also the horrors of the trenches (p. 25/20) are summed up in terms of wardrobe.

Stoppard came across Carr when researching Joyce; his other discovery was that while in Zurich Joyce had staged a production of Earnest. This must have been exciting for a dramatist who admits to difficulty in thinking up plots, and who had already had success constructing one play around Hamlet and another (The Real Inspector Hound, 1968) round the formula of a country-house murder-mystery. Earnest is not only written by the ultimate dandy, Oscar Wilde, whose style Stoppard partly admired, it is also the one play which might conceivably be even more familiar to London audiences than *Hamlet* itself.

Background Text:
The Importance of Being Earnest

Since its first performance in 1895, Wilde's comedy has been a mainstay not only of professional theatre but also of amateur drama at all levels; so skilfully is it crafted that even the clumsiest performers can make something of it. *Earnest* combines an ingenious plot with an elegant epigrammatic style which echoed the late-seventeenth-century plays of William Congreve, but which was also, in its deliberate paradoxes and reversals, particularly characteristic of the 1890s. The play also exemplifies at its best the style of 'camp' – a gleefully 'over the top' performance, parodying or exaggerating tradition. Camp is theatrical, but has also influenced the performance style of many rock stars. It often hints at homosexuality, appropriately enough in Wilde's case. Recently a suggestion has been made that the very word 'earnest' may have been 1890s code for 'homosexual'; if so the title would be quite brazen to those in the know. But even the usual meaning of 'earnest' – sincere and serious – is ironically different from the attitudes found in this play.

Ernest (without the 'a') was a fairly common Christian name in Victorian times.

Synopsis of *Earnest* (as needed for *Travesties*)
Jack is a foundling adopted by a wealthy gentleman who, at his death, left him to be guardian of his daughter Cecily at his country house. In order to get up to London, Jack has invented a brother Ernest; once in London, he himself

lives as Ernest, is the friend of Algernon, and the boyfriend of Algernon's cousin Gwendolen (who is particularly in love with Ernest's *name*).

In the first act, Algernon delightedly discovers Jack's deception and also the address of Cecily. Jack is grilled as a possible husband by Gwendolen's mother, Lady Bracknell, but is dismissed because he has no parents.

In the second act Algernon appears at the country house passing himself off as Ernest. Cecily is delighted; she has fantasised about meeting him (she particularly loves his *name*) and has even agreed, in spite of his complete ignorance of her existence, to marry him. Algernon is startled but happy to agree. When Jack arrives, he dare not expose Algernon. Gwendolen then appears, curious to know more about her Ernest's life in the country; and is displeased to find a pretty eighteen-year-old there, moreover one who also claims to be engaged to Ernest. While preserving the utmost social poise, elegantly taking afternoon tea in the presence of servants, they contrive to be extremely rude to each other. But when Jack and Algernon appear, each is recognised by his relative and greeted by his true name. Ernest does not exist, therefore neither Gwendolen nor Cecily is engaged to be married to anyone. They embrace each other in deep sympathy.

In the third act, Lady Bracknell arrives in pursuit of her daughter. She is surprised to find her nephew also there, particularly when he announces he wants to marry Cecily. Since Cecily stands to inherit wealth, Lady Bracknell gives her consent to the marriage; but Jack refuses to give his until Lady Bracknell agrees to his own marriage with Gwendolen.

At this point Cecily's governess, Miss Prism, is recognised by Lady Bracknell. Prism was the nursemaid who, twenty-eight years ago, muddling the infant Jack with the manuscript of a novel, lost him and fled. Jack is actually Algernon's elder brother, and had been christened Ernest. Both couples are ecstatic; and two minor characters, Miss Prism and the local rector, Dr Chasuble, also seem headed for marital bliss.

Wilde's light-hearted play deals with dangerous material. Victorian society was prudish to the point of perverseness – cloth frills were put round piano legs, because they were *legs*! Yet human nature had not changed; and the male double-life – keeping a mistress in town, or regularly visiting prostitutes – seems to have been socially acceptable amongst men and rarely challenged by women. There was still sanctimonious scandal, however, if such behaviour by a prominent citizen was discovered. The eleventh commandment was 'Thou shalt not be found out.'

Earnest managed to be suitable for twelve-year-olds, while at the same time tapping into the excitement of such peril. It seems likely that most London audiences, even while laughing at Jack's second identity as Ernest, were aware of the less amusing social realities hinted at. And some at least will also have known that Wilde himself, a forty-one-year-old married man with two children, had been leading a double life with rent boys and an increasingly open affair with an aristocrat in his early twenties, Lord Alfred Douglas. Ten years earlier, all homosexual acts had been made illegal. In February 1895, *Earnest* was a huge success; a few months later, Wilde was in prison after being publicly accused by Douglas's father. In hindsight, the play seems to have been simultaneously harmless and outrageous – pushing its author's luck.

Travesties, however, does not exploit this particular excitement. Stoppard uses Wilde's play rather the other way: as a stable and innocent outline, a structure of classical English decorum, which can itself be travestied as much as historical figures such as Joyce.

In early drafts, Stoppard's play was called *Prism*, after Cecily's governness, whose name suggests both primness and toughness. A prism shows light at different angles and from different sides: and that is the kind of multiple vision offered by the crazy arguments in Act One of *Travesties*, and also more uneasily by the excerpts from Lenin in Act Two.

The scheme of *Earnest*

Stoppard's project was always going to be wild and unhistorical. Tzara started Dada in 1916, Lenin took the train to St Petersburg early in 1917 and Joyce's production of *Earnest* was not until 1918. *Travesties* disclaims any pretence at historical accuracy, initially by being framed within the conspicuously senile mind of Old Carr, part memory part fantasy, but also by simultaneously offering itself as a travesty of *Earnest*. How Stoppard designed this, and also what he decided not to do, is worth study.

Algernon would obviously be represented by Carr, as he was in Joyce's production. Jack, the double-living young hero, would therefore fall to the young dandy Tzara. Stoppard says that only after he had mentally 'cast' Tzara thus did he discover that the actor who played Jack in Joyce's production had shared Tzara's first name, Tristan. A similar but more astonishing coincidence, again discovered after the basic 'casting' had been decided, was that Joyce, who was to fit very approximately into the role of Lady Augusta Bracknell, had himself in error been registered at birth as 'Augusta' rather than 'Augustine' (see p. 30/24).

Thus a very rough kind of equation could be proposed between three 'historical' (though travestied) men and three characters from Wilde. In the cases of Cecily and Gwendolen the process went into reverse: characters from *Earnest* were imported into Stoppard's travesty of history, to become the assistants of Lenin and Joyce. This results in a somewhat marginal part for Gwen, but a particularly strong one for Cecily. Bennett – in Carr's fantasy-memory the name of a servant – could stand in both for Lane in Algernon's London flat and Merriman in Jack's country house. On the other hand, and significantly, no attempt was made to include the Lenins. 'I felt very strongly ... that one thing I could not do was to integrate the Lenins in the *Importance* scheme' (to Hayman).

The synopsis and commentary below indicate by italics where and how Stoppard's play follows Wilde's. They also reveal how Lenin is kept apart.

Travesties: Synopsis and Commentary

Act One

Joyce, Tzara and Lenin (with Gwen) are working in the Zurich Public Library. At first there is silence. Tzara then cuts up what he has written and reads the scraps out apparently at random; the result is gibberish, except that it happens to make sense in French. Fragments of Joyce's work are also heard aloud, and also seem gibberish. The librarian, Cecily, shushes them. Gwen receives a folder from Joyce, and Cecily one from Lenin; and the folders are accidentally exchanged. (*This is a very minor, travesty version of the exchange of baby and manuscript twenty-eight years before the start of* Earnest.)

Tzara leaves. So do Gwen and Cecily, taking the wrong folders with them. Nadya bursts into the library (p. 3/3) and tells Lenin that a revolution has started in St Petersburg; all this is in Russian, while Joyce declaims incomprehensible notes. Lenin drops a scrap of paper which Joyce reads aloud: English words of Marxist abuse. (In the 1974 version they were statistics of capitalist profit.) Joyce returns the scrap to Lenin, who tries different languages on him; Joyce responds to each in turn. The Lenins leave, and the prologue ends with a limerick and a song, the limerick being a trap set by Joyce for Cecily, who completes it when intending to curtail it.

This prologue is like a Stoppard play in miniature. The audience is teased by an opening silence, then by an absurd action, then by a varied flow of language, all of it incomprehensible. Though actually practising their art, Joyce and Tzara appear like clowns, with Gwen and Cecily as their foils. Lenin, however, appears intensely serious.

The scene changes to the Room, scene of Old Carr's reminiscences. During six pages (pp. 6–11/5–9) of meandering, with many erratic shifts suggesting that he is an unreliable witness, he reveals that he was a consular official in Zurich, that he knew Joyce, Lenin and the Dadaists, and that he acted in a production of *Earnest*.

At the foot of p. 11/9, Old Carr becomes young Carr in his drawing room, and his servant Bennett brings him tea things. Pages 12–18/10–15 skilfully bridge us into the

Earnest scheme. We begin with Carr's relief at being away from the trenches, and his curious 'time slips' (see stage note on p. 13/11) enable a repeated update of the situation in Russia. Bennett resembles P. G. Wodehouse's Jeeves in having a total and dispassionate command of events. *A sudden direct quotation from* Earnest *(p. 15/13, 'eight bottles of champagne ...') links us to the opening of Wilde's play; it is a deft link because the line implies servants taking advantage of their masters, and the main news is of class conflict in Russia.*

On p. 18/15, the non-Wilde subplot begins: a telegram from 'the Minister' urges Carr to 'ascertain Lenin's plans'. Tzara then enters *as Wilde's Jack*, although loudly un-English, followed almost instantly by Gwen and Joyce. Gwen proves to be Carr's sister (*as Gwendolen is Algernon's*) but otherwise the ensuing 'manic' sequence of limericks (pp. 19–23/16–18) does not correspond to anything in *Earnest*. Joyce introduces himself to Carr and Tzara and invites Carr to act in his play, and Tzara's Dadaist antics are mentioned, against which Carr asserts 'British culture', his example being Gilbert and Sullivan's *Iolanthe*.

For one line (p. 23/19) the lights are dim and Old Carr is alone again with his memories – though the line actually completes the final previous limerick. Then the lights go up: we see Bennett and young Carr again, and for the second time Tzara enters as Jack (*we are back once more to the second page of* Earnest), but this time Tzara speaks Wildean English. They argue, Tzara expounding his Dadaist rejection of history, traditional art and patriotism, Carr angrily remembering his war experiences. On p. 29/23 the memory overwhelms him, the lights growing dim to the sound of a song from the trenches: it is another glimpse of Old Carr. Then the lights return and *we see for a third time Tzara's entry as Jack. Carr/Algernon learns of the existence of Cecily, and that Tzara/Jack is here to propose to Gwendolen.* On p. 32/26 Carr realises the identity of the 'Joyce' he has assumed to be a female chaperone for his sister (*the first hint that Joyce is to correspond to Gwendolen's mother, Lady Bracknell*).

The Earnest *scheme continues as Carr produces Tzara's library ticket, which is in the name of Jack. The explanation (p. 34/28) is that Tzara was avoiding Lenin's known hostility to the Dadaist Tristan – hastily described by Tzara as 'my younger brother'. Carr/Algernon notes Cecily's 'address' – the reference section – though unlike Algernon his interest in her is not yet amorous: she represents his chance to spy out Lenin's plans.* For a second time Tzara and Carr argue about art. On p. 37/29 Gwen and Joyce enter (again) and the material of pp. 19–23/16–18 is roughly repeated in rather less lunatic manner – though for one instant on p. 38/30 a limerick does threaten to overtake the dialogue. On pp. 42–3/33–4 Joyce shrewdly interests Carr by references to the costumes Algernon will wear, and they leave to 'peruse' the play.

Jack's courtship of Gwendolen is now paralleled by Tzara's of Gwen, pp. 44–7/34–7; this includes a Shakespeare sonnet which when cut up becomes sexually suggestive. Gwen reveals that she was attracted to Tzara because he admired Joyce as an artist; since he actually doesn't, this corresponds to Gwendolen's enthusiasm for Jack's name of Ernest. As they embrace, Joyce enters with Lady Bracknell's line – 'Rise, sir ...' Gwen gives Tzara a folder containing what she believes to be a chapter of *Ulysses* (actually, see p. 3/3, a chapter by Lenin) in the form of the Christian catechism. She leaves, and the catechetical form is indeed followed as *Joyce/Lady Bracknell interviews Tzara/Jack. Where Lady B. enquires about Jack's* parents, *Joyce enquires about* Dada. (*Ouch.*) At the start of the interrogation Joyce's hair was covered with cut-up scraps of Shakespeare (Tzara had been using Joyce's hat on p. 44/35); during it he replaces these in the hat, then (p. 51/45) Joyce conjures from it a white carnation, followed by handkerchiefs and flags. Eventually he cannot resist a joke at Dada's expense, and Tzara erupts with anger, an eruption similar in form to those of Carr against Tzara himself on p. 28/22 and Tzara against Carr on p. 36/28. He accuses Joyce of having 'turned literature into a religion'. Joyce begins his reply more calmly, but it becomes an eloquent defence of the immortality of art which nevertheless will 'leave the world precisely as it finds it' – art, that is, for art's sake. He ends (p. 54/42) powerfully, *with an echo of Lady Bracknell*. Each of the three expatriates, Tzara, Joyce and Carr, has now been on the receiving end of a sustained speech of attack by one of the others. Lenin, of course, has not, and is by now half forgotten, since he left the stage on p. 5/4.

The Earnest *scheme has now reached the end of Wilde's Act One*. Stoppard's act ends in Old Carr's reminiscences about his feud with Joyce and his later dream that he asked Joyce 'what did you do in the Great War?' and was told: 'I wrote *Ulysses*. What did you do?'

Act Two
Intervals are significant elements in an evening at the theatre. Here, the audience is very probably delighted, if 'sometimes finding it hard to follow'; and perhaps a bit

pleased with itself – this is a smart play which demands some framework of knowledge. The first act has also included some eloquent defences of 'playing', so by having paid for their seats people can feel they have subscribed to the glory of art as outlined by Joyce. What is more, there are still two acts of Wilde's comedy left to be travestied.

'I thought it would be quite nice,' Stoppard has admitted, 'if they all went out thinking "oh this is fun isn't it", came back, and [I] just hit them with this boring thing, as though they'd come back into the wrong theatre.' In his original script, Cecily was there already when they returned, a teacher waiting for everyone to settle down, and the lecture that followed started with the publication of *Das Kapital* in 1872 and lasted for five lengthy pages. 'I remember thinking I might be pushing my luck.' Gradually, at rehearsal, the lecture was short-ened – though it remained complete in the published script, and at a production in Paris the entire lecture was apparently performed to totally attentive audiences, the director having decided that Cecily should be naked. The 1993 version preserves only the final section of the lecture, and makes substantial other alterations which diminish the heaviness with which Lenin originally landed on the comedy of the play, almost crushing the life out of it.

And yet there should be some shock-effect. The lecture is humourless, on a humourless subject. When, on p. 58/ 46, the Lenins re-enact their urgent conversation in the library, Cecily 'pedantically repeats each speech in English'. It is as if we are meant to be bored – and perhaps a bit alarmed. The ground-rules seem also to have shifted: we thought the play was taking place within the memories of Old Carr, and then within the scheme of

Earnest; but now we seem to have lost both of those comfortable frameworks.

But then Carr enters, reassuringly – we aren't going to be trapped within the grim story of Russia and Lenin. Carr's 'manner betrays' that he is now a spy – presumably he does some caricature slinking-around. And when Cecily sees him we are *suddenly paralleling Act Two of* Earnest. *Carr uses Tzara's visiting card (see p. 14/12) to pass himself off as 'Jack's decadent nihilist younger brother'.* Their conversation, while loosely following the flirtation in Wilde, shows Carr attempting to discover Lenin's movements, reveals that Bennett is a socialist who routinely passes consular letters to Tzara, and also refers to the Zurich production of *Earnest* – which in turn triggers Cecily's insistence on a Marxist view of art. *Like Algernon, Carr asks Cecily to reform him* (p. 61/50) – she gives him a folder to read, which she believes contains an article by Lenin but (see p. 3/3) actually contains a chapter by Joyce. Carr, however, launches (p. 65/51) into a surprisingly well-informed insistence that 'Marx got it wrong'. He attempts to return to Wilde by comparing Cecily to '*a pink rose*', but she tells him, in most un-Wildean terms, that this is 'because I'm about to puke', and treats him to a harangue similar in shape to the three previously heard on pp. 28, 37 and 53/22, 29 and 41. During it, however, Carr begins mentally to undress her and this view is hilariously shared by the audience (stage directions, p. 66/52).

Carr's erotic frenzy is abruptly ended by a return to normal lighting and a third re-use of *Cecily's line, 'I don't think you ought to talk to me like that ...'* *She reveals that she has always wanted to love Jack's decadent nihilist younger brother ... and drags him down behind her desk*

(p. 67/53). The Lenins enter, with their serious history: Carr, as spy, is seen eavesdropping. *Tzara enters as Jack and we are again into Wilde's scheme*; but the Lenins – in an excellent stage-moment emphasising their incompatibility with the laughter – 'stop and stare at these events' (p. 69/54).

Momentarily, in a 1993 addition, the Lenins are brought into the comedy, being required to shake hands with Tristan/Carr – but they remain 'stunned', and leave, as does Cecily. Tzara and Carr find themselves back in Carr's room, *arguing, like Jack and Algernon, over muffins*; simultaneously, from another part of the stage, we hear the build-up to Lenin's departure by train for St Petersburg. This is shorter than in the original; also the sequence of stage events has been altered. Too late, Carr is seen insisting that 'he must be stopped' (p. 73/57).

The stage goes black except for a light on Lenin. He is seen as fierce public orator, modelled upon a famous photograph. Stoppard's original stage-note reads: '*It is structurally important to the act that the following speech is delivered from the strongest possible position with the most dramatic change of effect.*' And the original speech began with his grim harangue (now p. 75/58), 'Today, literature ...' But in the 1993 version, in a fundamental strategic shift, Lenin here starts with *lines from Wilde*: '*really ... carelessness!*'

There follows a speech by Carr in which he implies that he might have stopped Lenin travelling (and thus changed the course of twentieth-century history) but was distracted from doing so by his 'feelings for Cecily'. He remains on stage as the next four pages are dominated by the Lenins' writings; again there are substantial changes here from the original, and in a dry new twist Carr, on pp. 76–7/60–1, repeatedly agrees with Lenin about art. At the top of p. 79/61, Carr even feels he might have got on far better with Lenin than he did with Tzara or Joyce. Perhaps ignorant bourgeois philistinism is not so fundamentally different from totalitarian socialism.

Carr drops out on p. 79/62 as the Lenin material comes to a climax. Lenin is quoted being deeply moved by Beethoven, and yet rejecting 'such beauty'; instead, 'we've got to hit heads'. Nadya recalls a past failure of communication with her husband which nevertheless resonates through all we have heard of her memories: 'Something went wrong. I forget what.' This is arguably the play's most serious line, though finely understated. Then Beethoven's music swells past it.

That is the last of the Lenins in this play; and, since it is by Stoppard, 'minus A' is more than due. Beethoven 'degenerates absurdly' into a 1920s music routine, and *a verse travesty of the classic Gwendolen/Cecily confrontation in* Earnest *(pp. 81–4/62–6). The true identities of Tzara and Carr are then revealed, to the young women's mutual disappointment*; and (p. 85/67) they are asked for their true opinions of the chapters they read. They have to admit having concealed those opinions because of their love – *just as Wilde's characters preserved their false names because of love*. But, privately, both thought the chapters drivel.

Carr tackles Tzara, amicably, about Bennett's leaking of Consular correspondence. It is Bennett's victory, just as Lenin may be winning in Russia – far from being censured, he is merely allowed more champagne; and indeed *the Perriet-Jouet, Brut, '89* is 'all gone' – 'the writing on the wall' (p. 87/68) heralding the collapse of class privilege. Very belatedly – he has been forgotten for the whole act, so far – Joyce returns to conduct his quarrel with Carr, followed by the revelation of *the inadvertent folders-swop* and a resultant blissful reconciliation, ending – as in many traditional comedies – in a dance (p. 90/70). Finally, Old Carr and Old Cecily are left dancing on stage, and the falseness of Carr's recollections is admitted. Nothing that we have heard can be historically trusted: it has been a travesty.

The Problem of Lenin

Some early criticisms of *Travesties* seemed to think Stoppard might not have *noticed* that Lenin didn't fit into its humour: careless of him. The above synopsis shows the opposite: in the first scene Lenin is presented at the key moment of his life, urgent and serious, but then is allowed to drift out of our thoughts, so that his later impact will be that much more jarring. There is some shift of emphasis in the 1993 revisions, but even now the main weight of Act Two lies between pp. 67/53 and 79/62. 'The second act,' Stoppard has said, 'is Lenin's act really.' 'The problem of Lenin' is one of the play's main topics.

We may think the problem might just as well have been Hitler (from whom Stoppard's family fled) or Stalin; any fanatical leader who tyrannises a vast populace could reveal the limitations of Joyce's art-for-art's sake, Tzara's Dadaism, or Carr's stale Englishness. But Lenin was the one who was in Zurich where they were: that was the coincidence which set the whole play going. And Lenin of all historical figures is the one who seems to have preoccupied Stoppard most at the time: in January 1974, when *Travesties* had been written but not yet performed, he introduced Lenin's name into his interview with *Theatre Quarterly* and proceeded:

> in the ten years after 1917 fifty times more people were done to death than in the *fifty years* before 1917 ... Lenin perverted Marxism, and Stalin carried on from there. When one reads pre-revolutionary Lenin, notably *What is to be Done?* but also all the letters and articles in which he railed against the early Marxists who had the temerity to disagree with him, one can see with awful clarity that ideological differences are often temperamental differences in ideological disguise – and also that the terror to come was implicit in the Lenin of 1900.

The strangeness of *Travesties* comes partly from the fact that Stoppard determined to include Lenin onstage *alongside*, yet *not part of*, a glittering burlesque; and then from the fact that he chose *not* to fictionalise him. The Acknowledgements (p. xiii/xii) insist: 'Nearly everything spoken by Lenin and Nadezhda Krupskaya herein comes from his Collected Writings and from her *Memories of Lenin*.'

In other words, a major role in the play, and substantial portions of its theatre time, are not scripted by Stoppard at all. Wearing protective gloves, he lifts them from elsewhere and dumps them with a kind of shudder into the farcical flow; which they almost manage to stop. But why? Why do it? The intention can hardly have been to write an anti-Lenin play – if anything, it was rather to write one that was pro-Joyce. Nor can Stoppard have simply found he hadn't the stomach to write about Lenin – that would have produced a marginalised character, perhaps an obvious clown with little relation to reality, not one to whom he decided to give the weight of the second act.

An answer of sorts seems to come a little later in the *Theatre Quarterly* interview, in what has become a famous sentence. Stoppard has just been talking about the fact that art rarely has short-term effects, cannot usually reverse political wrongs; it works in the long term. Art, he says, 'provides the moral matrix, the moral sensibility, from which we make our judgments about the world'.

Allowing Lenin into *Travesties* enlarged the play's 'moral matrix', broadened its range and its seriousness. The idea is perhaps an extension of 'A, but minus A'. Since Stoppard evidently has much sympathy with the climactic speech of Joyce on p. 53/41–2, praising 'art that leaves the world precisely as it finds it', it may be realistic and responsible of him to set against it the fact of Lenin – and then almost to allow Lenin to win, in terms of our evening in the theatre. In his final speech (p. 79/62) Lenin comes startlingly close to Joyce; the Appassionata is 'superhuman ... it makes me feel proud of the miracles that human beings can perform'. But then he decides this feeling must be fought down. At this moment – the only time we glimpse his personal rather than public feelings – Lenin appears human, sincere – and yet perverted.

However unconsciously, Stoppard may have had some political intention. His next serious plays would be about dissidents under Communist regimes; part of the shock-effect of Lenin was to remind the comfortable London audience of the tyrannies still continuing further east. And the collapse of Communist regimes in Russia and Eastern Europe in the late 1980s may be one reason why the 1993 version of the play softens the impact of Lenin – as if it feels it can *afford* to.

The 1993 revisions

Most of the changes are reductions. Cecily's lecture was cut in performance from the start, and is now a fraction of its original length, and merely slightly disconcerting. For five pages of the original, Nadya and Lenin were the only characters onstage, alternating chunks of the memoirs and letters; now Old Carr is onstage with them, the framing chorus figure, commenting and – a real ironic surprise – actually agreeing at times. Seen this way, Lenin is a lot less alarming – is more the man whose statues now lie in ruins.

These seem reasonable tactical decisions, very probably assisted by discussions with actors and directors: the revised script is probably more user-friendly for everyone. What seems more questionable in the 1993 version is a perfunctory attempt to link Lenin with the comedy. Admittedly in the original there was allowable audience laughter at Lenin's genuinely proposed stratagems – the wig and the Swedish deaf mutes. But now on p. 67/53 he turns up in clerical dress and the stage-note attempts to relate him in some way to Canon Chasuble in Wilde – and, with even less reason, Nadya to Miss Prism. This is probably lost on the audience, and none of the pleasantly amusing characteristics of Chasuble and Prism can ever be hinted at. The most significant change occurs on p. 74/58, where Lenin's public oratory, clearly intended in the original production to be fairly awe-inspiring (see synopsis, this book p. 122), now begins with lines lifted from Wilde: 'Really, if the lower orders ...' and 'To lose one revolution ... ' In 1993, this was more likely to produce laughter than awe. Certainly the lines from Wilde are lifted with skill, proving grimly appropriate: Lenin was indeed relying on 'the lower orders' to put him into power, and the 1905 revolution had indeed been lost. But this late decision to taint Lenin with Wilde, and Wilde with Lenin, seems to blur a basic principle of the play's original structure; indeed, to Hayman in 1974 Stoppard insisted, 'it would have been disastrous to Prismize and Chasublize the Lenins'. See also the quotation in this book p. 115.

At one other point the 1993 version is significantly altered: Cecily's stripper-act (p. 66/52). After the mid-page stage-notes ('Faintly ... at this point') the original text read:

> In England the rich own the poor and the men own the women. Five per cent of the people own eighty per cent of the property. The only way is the way of Marx, and of Lenin, the enemy of all revisionism – of economism – opportunism – liberalism – of bourgeois anarchist individualism – of quasi-socialist ad-hoc-ism, of syndicalist quasi-Marxist populism – liberal quasi-communist opportunism, economist quasi-internationalist imperialism, social chauvinist quasi-Zimmervaldist Menshevism, self-determinist quasi-socialist annexationism, Kautskyism, Bundism, Kantism –

The statistics about inequality in England jabbed briefly at the affluent audience. Then Cecily's '-isms' carried a faint reminiscence of Polonius introducing the Players in *Hamlet*: ('pastoral-comical, historical-pastoral, tragical-historical, tragical-comical-historical-pastoral') – in both cases the absurd list damaging the credibility of both its subject and its speaker. Cecily's (and Lenin's) political commitment, persuasive a moment earlier, was shown degenerating – by a degeneration of *language* – into insane fanaticism. It seemed one of the best strokes of the play. But in 1993 the emphasis shifts to issues of art, where Cecily's assertions simply contradict the socialist line she was taking on p. 66/50; and her speech finally collapses into the feeble and tasteless joke, 'rheumatism', where previously a good satirical point was being made.

Stagecraft

Pigs' breakfasts and ambushes

Stoppard the craftsman offered a characteristically frank assessment to Ronald Hayman in the year *Travesties* was first peformed, 1974:

> *Jumpers* and *Travesties* are very similar plays ... they're so similar that were I to do it a third time it would be a bore. You start with a prologue which is slightly strange. Then you have an interminable monologue which is rather funny. Then you have scenes. Then you end up with another monologue. And you have unexpected bits of music and dance, and at the same time people are playing ping-pong with various intellectual arguments ... there are senses in which *Travesties* is a great advance on *Jumpers*, but it's the same kind of pig's breakfast.

Pigs are not fussy what they eat, or how it's served up. This is not a man inclined to over-praise his own work, or to claim any mystical inspiration. And incidentally, no, he never *has* tried to repeat the formula of these two plays.

Elsewhere Stoppard has said (of *Jumpers*, but it applies equally to *Travesties*) that it 'breaks its neck to be entertaining', and that his aim has been to try to put something of theatrical interest – generally comic – into every moment. He also talked of 'contriving the perfect marriage between the play of ideas and farce'. Such phrasing – especially 'breaks its neck' and 'contriving' – emphasises how consciously manufactured these plays are. In all their brilliance, they can continue to feel like bits stuck together, rather than a single piece which has grown steadily and naturally from a strong story-line (as usually happens in more realist drama). The *entertainment* level is for some spectators much higher than their final level of *satisfaction*.

A favourite word of the young Stoppard was 'ambush'. In an ambush people are led for a while along an apparently safe route, then subjected to a surprise attack. Stoppard is quite capable of ambushing his audience even in a play's opening moments, having led them unsuspecting into the theatre: at least three of his plays, including *Travesties*, begin with baffling mixtures of language. It is some relief to arrive at the comprehensible narrative of Old Carr on p. 6/5, but then that route soon starts to feel insecure as his mind and language wander. When Bennett enters (p. 11/9) there is hope of a story, a *play*, developing; but on p. 15/11 it seems ambushed by a time-slip – Bennett and Carr repeating lines from a page earlier – and in the next few pages by several more. The entrance of Tzara, Gwen and Joyce on pp. 18–19/15 seems (oh, that's better) to signal the travesty of *Earnest* hinted at by earlier echoes ('eight bottles of champagne are entered …'); but it instantly then crashes, Tzara appearing as a ludicrous foreigner and the dialogue locked into idiot limericks; hopes of Wildean elegance are dashed almost as soon as raised. But then, p. 23/19, suddenly the whole Tzara entrance is re-staged and the speeches become Wildean prose after all: ah, what a relief. (It is

entirely characteristic of Stoppard to present the more
ridiculous version *first*, where almost any other script-
writer would instinctively escalate his absurdities.) And so
on. The play rides off on its own breathtaking roller-
coaster, which by the end of Act One we have just about
got used to, having learned to hold on tight, and blink and
gasp and laugh. But then of course comes Act Two, and
the dour, unfunny ambush of Cecily's lecture: see above,
'The Problem of Lenin' ... On pp. 71–9/56–60 (and even
more so in the original version) some in the audience must
wonder whether all the earlier part of the evening has just
been luring them here, to this suddenly dark cold place.
But no: after the cold and darkness and Beethoven's music
have been worked into a tense theatrical climax (p. 80/
62), Beethoven himself is suddenly ambushed by a 1920s
song-and-dance routine ... The last words of the play are
its final ambush: 'I learned three things ... I forget the
third thing.'

All Stoppard's drama uses this pattern of deception
and surprise; but *Travesties* most of all, and it seems
appropriate that this is the play which includes a
conjuring act – since conjuring depends to a great
extent on diversionary techniques, leading the attention
astray. In studying the crafting of this play we are
studying the calculated shuffling about of different cards.
Each is an idea of interest in itself; but whether any of
them is really *developed* in the course of the play may be
questioned. What *Travesties* offers, whether as entertainment or as mental challenge, is more the juxtaposition,
the bringing-alongside, of disparate ingredients than their
blending towards any growth or resolution.

Some of these 'cards' might be identified as follows:

- Old Carr's monologues – pp. 6–11, 29, 54–6, 74, 91–2/ 5–11, 23, 42–44, 58, 71. These introduce and touch on most of the other 'cards'.
- the scheme of *Earnest* – see italics on pp. 116–124 in this book.
- the debate about Art – pp. 25–8, 35–6, 51–4, 63–4, 75– 9/20–21, 28–9, 41–2, 49–50, 58–62.
- the debate about Communism – pp. 16–17, 65–6/13–14, 50–52.
- the debates about patriotism, war and history – pp. 24– 8/19–23.
- Russian history and writings by the Lenins – pp. 15–18, 57–8, 61, 67–9, 71–9/12–15, 45–6, 48, 53–4, 56–62.
- games with language – pp. 2–5, 6–12/2–4, 5–11 (Carr's slips and puns), 19–23, 44–6, 48–53/16–18, 30, 35–6, 38–41 (catechism), 64/50 (titles as insults), 67/52 (-isms), 81–6/62–6; and the pattern of explosive speeches (28, 36, 53, 65–6/22, 29, 41–2, 51–2).

Characters

With the exception of the final quotation from Lenin himself (p. 79/62), psychological realism is not attempted in *Travesties*. Carr's recollections are the nearest we get to it. His memories of the trenches and his relief at being in Switzerland are sketched convincingly enough, as is the mixture of grudge and frustrated self-importance in his various attempts at 'memoirs'. But his obsession with fine tailoring is taken to cartoon extremes – which entirely fits the general tone of the play.

Lenin is seen mostly externally and allowed to speak for himself; as noted above, Stoppard chose not to *write* him. The rest of the characters are farce stereotypes, not even close copies of Wilde's characters, and are expected to perform at different times in quite different modes – limerick backchat, impassioned speech, song-and-dance: they are basically the leads in a musical revue. Their claims on our more serious attention rest in the unfarcical beliefs some of them defend – which is why Gwen, who is given no intellectual stance, gets somewhat squeezed out.

Collectively, the characters of *Travesties* are strikingly different from those in most other Stoppard plays. Typically, he writes about relative innocents – about Moons more than Malquists (see p. 18 of this book) – people muddling through life wishing no ill to others and even trying, as best they can, to behave decently. This reasonably describes Ros and Guil in *Rosencrantz*, and Dotty, George, Bones and Crouch in *Jumpers*. They are people who are unsure of many things, but muck along anyway – and who go on asking moral questions. The characters of *Travesties*, on the other hand, radiate a staggering, sometimes alarming, self-confidence. They have *arrived* at their beliefs and don't propose to be budged from them. This doesn't include Nadya, and Gwen remains a bit marginal, and Old Carr's erratic memories carry hints of pathetic self-doubt; but young Carr, Tzara, Joyce, Cecily and Lenin are all given speeches of ranting ideological certainty. And even Bennett, as a secret doctrinaire socialist who on his final appearance looks at his employer 'implacably' (p. 87/68), prides himself on his knowingness: he is sure, like the others, that he *has it right*. Their dialogue, modelled as it is on Wilde, is superficially dandyish and cynical; but when provoked these characters turn out not to be cynics at all, but more like fanatics.

Stoppard wants them heard and he wants us to care –

not for them as characters but for the ideas they declaim: about the horror of the trenches, about the commercial and political amoralities that led to that horror, about whether there is a 'natural right of the people to the common ownership of their country and its resources', about the 'false premise ... that people are a sensational kind of material object', about the absurdity and gratuitousness of art, and about its necessity and immortality. But what the play will not do is settle for one of these views at the expense of the others. At the beginning and end, and in the brief refuelling stop at the end of Act One, our only grounding is in Old Carr: there is little risk of our being tempted suddenly to take up the position of any single one of these 'knowers'. For all Stoppard's admitted sympathy with Joyce's position, this remains a play in which 'Tom Stoppard Doesn't Know.' More than that, it seems to offer a comic caution against those who claim too fervently that they do.

Textual Notes

Act One

1/1 *The play* ... – note the directions of the experienced dramatist: on a few things he needs to insist, on others (see The LIBRARY) he tries to be as flexible as possible.

2/2 The first minutes of the play are deliberately baffling, denying us any conventional dialogue in English. A bewildering jumble of languages surrounds an urgent conversation in Russian. The multi-lingual setting of Zurich is established, as is the multi-national cast. The

elaborate difficulty and fragmentation of much
Modernist literature are also suggested.

Tzara's first four lines – a random 'found'
poem made after cutting up a previous piece of
writing – becomes a limerick in French. It
seems to go something like this:

Il est un homme, s'appelle Tzara
Qui des richesses a-t-il le nonpareil [??]
Il reste a la Suisse
Parce qu'il est un artiste
'Nous n'avons que l'art', il declara.

Translated back into English this might be: 'The
man called Tzara, of unparalleled talents, stays
in Switzerland as an artist, declaring that all that
matters is Art.' Nothing could be a better
introduction to the themes of the play – if the
audience understood it.

So should the actor speak it in fluent French,
emphasising the limerick structure? Or should he
read it word by English word in puzzlement, and
hope at least some of the audience will
nevertheless hear the French meaning and the
poetic form? Or does the whole thing remain a
private joke between dramatist and someone
who *reads* the printed play?
Deshill holles eamus – the three lines which
Joyce dictates are indeed repeated thrice, and
form the opening incantation of Chapter XIV of
Joyce's *Ulysses*, a chapter which (see p. 90/70)
'uses the gamut of English literature from
Chaucer to Carlyle'. The scene is a maternity
hospital in Dublin (p. 90/70 again: 'remotely

connected with midwifery'); in this first line
Joyce's concoction is actually pre-Chaucer,
suggesting Old English and Latin as well as the
location, Holles Street.

— Send us ... wombfruit – send us a child: an
invocation to the Sun (but the hospital's boss is
a man called Horne).

— Hoopsa ... – joyfully the midwife lifts the baby,
which is a boy.

4/3 *scraps* – I haven't been able to locate these in
Ulysses or elsewhere. Again, the words come
from several languages, with hints ('Aquinas'
and 'consubstantiality') of Joyce's Catholic
upbringing.

5/4 'Lickspittle ... – Lenin is preparing the propaganda which Bennett will quote on p. 17/14.

— *Declaims* – i.e., like a big speech. '*Silence!*' is
here in French, therefore roughly rhymes with
'response'. This offence against the library's
rule is also what the limerick is about; and
Cecily herself completes it as she tries to stop it
('ssssssh!').

6/5 If you ever ... – a popular Irish song; Joyce
was a talented singer.

— not actually from Limerick – the town gave its
name to the form of poem.

— Not a great patron ... – there is a strong echo
in these lines of 'Pete' in the 'Dud and Pete'
sketches of the English humorist Peter Cook.

7/6 do it on my head – is Old Carr's admission that
punning comes only too easily to him. Not all
his puns and references are noted below. The
main comic points of the speech are (a) its

frenzied energy: all this has been bottled up for a long time; and (b) its repeated contradictions: for example, Joyce 'exhibited a monkish unconcern for worldly and bodily comforts' but a moment later was a 'fornicating drunk'. Of course Old Carr is indeed partly 'senile'; but also he is trying out different ways of composing his memoirs, to see how they sound: shall he aim to impress, or to tell the truth, or to vent his own frustrations?

– real blue ... empirical purple – 'empirical' means 'as real as we can tell from experience'; here with some pun on an emperor's purple?

– caviar for the general – (adapted from *Hamlet*); too rich for mass taste.

– *Elasticated Bloomers* – pun on the central character of *Ulysses*, Leopold Bloom; bloomers were women's loose trousers.

8/7 sponging – always borrowing money. snot-green – this charming comparison comes from the first section of *Ulysses*, where it is applied to the sea. It leads Old Carr to 'mucus mutandis', his variation on 'mutatis mutandis' (which means 'with the necessary changes').

– escapements – parts of watches or clocks (Switzerland's best-known industry). This leads to 'refugees' (who have 'escaped') and so to Lenin.

– astigmatic – suffering a defect of the eyes.

9/8 fine head ... clean-shaven – Lenin was dark, bald and bearded. A moment later Carr refers to a famous photograph of him speaking in Red Square, Moscow.

- comraderaderie – French *camaraderie* means a
  general matiness; but 'Comrade' (see p. 70/55)
  was the Communist standard form of address.
- Snowballs at all – echo of 'no balls at all' in the
  Second World War abusive song about Nazis.
- chagrinned – disappointed (to go with 'sadly'),
  pronounced 'sha-greened' (to replace 'snot-
  green').
- redlight district – i.e., containing brothels and
  sex shops, hence the puns which follow.

10/8 my art belongs ... – Carr alludes to a popular
  song, 'My Heart Belongs to Daddy' ('art' is a
  fruitful pun here) and to a famous First World
  War recruitment poster, 'What Did You Do in
  the Great War, Daddy?' The latter is echoed in
  the final words of this act, p. 56/44.

10/9 topographically – describing a place. This
  implies, absurdly, that the cliché 'high point'
  should be taken literally; thus 'snow' and
  'Alps'. Even before 'snow' Carr is thinking of
  'Where are the snows of yesteryear?', a well-
  known translation of a line by French poet
  François Villon – relevant here since it is a
  lament for youth past; and it later leads him to
  the outrageous pun 'the yes-no's of yesteryear'.
- Hugo Ball ... – Carr correctly remembers the
  names of leading Dadaists.
- sixpounders – cannon.
- howitzerland – gun. The point of the pun is
  that *Switzerland* in contrast was neutral and
  therefore safe.
- entente – understanding; 'détente' – relaxing of
  tension: both are terms from international

peace negotiations. Whereas 'to the left ... to the right ... into the valley' and 'blundered' are quotations from Tennyson's 'The Charge of the Light Brigade', about war at its worst and exceptionally high British casualties.

11/10 *bellicosity* – enthusiasm for war.

12/10 Bliss it was ... heaven – distorted from Wordsworth; 'Never in the whole history ...' distorted from Churchill.

– ora pro nobis – pray for us (to be saved from 'hell').

– asserted by a simple pin – comes from T. S. Eliot's *The Love Song of J. Alfred Prufrock*, the young Stoppard's favourite poem.

13/11 Savile Row – London street, the base for the classiest tailors.

– Hun ... Boche – First World War insulting names ('appellation') for Germans; but 'Bosh' also meant 'Rubbish', which is why Carr took offence.

– All Quiet on the Western Front – title of a novel by Erich Maria Remarque seeing the war from a German point of view.

14/11 tickety boo – all going well: here, refrain of a song from the trenches.

14/12 perfidy – (treachery) is by definition 'dishonest' and cannot be 'bona fide' (which means 'in good faith, straight').

– La Rochefoucauld – (1630–80) French statesman and writer of moral 'maxims'.

15/12 contraposed – opposed; 'fissiparous' – multiplying by splitting; 'disequilibrium' – imbalance. It is one of the oldest traditions in

European comedy that the servant may be cleverer than his master – or at least, as here and in P. G. Wodehouse, use longer words.

15/13 eight bottles of champagne – as on the first page of *Earnest*: this is the first of very few direct contacts with Wilde's play. The reversal of ideas in this speech – that aristocrats might revolt against their employees – is caricature-Wilde.

16/13 The Tsar – Bennett's long speech first gives a lightning update, then ruthlessly highlights the absurdity of dogma, which declares that this cannot be the real Revolution because Marx said it would take far longer. Marx saw Russia as more backward than Britain in its evolution towards the perfect Communist society; hence the end of the speech – Russia must go through the stage of British democracy.

17/14 free association – was indeed fashionable in psychoanalysis and in 'stream-of-consciousness' writing of the time. Carr means that 'artists' and 'riff-raff' made Bennett think of Tzara. (*Languidly*): I'm not sure ... – an echo of *Earnest*.

18/15 'Quel pays ... trous' – far from coming from La Rochefoucauld, this is a translation into French of Carr's p. 14/15 line, 'what a bloody country ... holes in it!'

– I ascertain Lenin's plans? – the spy-plot is introduced.

– If any doubt remained – the British Secret Service is bound to be wrong.

19/15 Plaizure ... marriage – a telescoping and
caricature of Algernon's early lines.

20/17 touch you – borrow money from you.

21/17 H.M.G. – His Majesty's Government.

– Cognoscenti – knowledgeable art-lovers.

22/18 *Iolanthe* – operetta by Gilbert and Sullivan, at
the height of popularity when Carr was
growing up.

– Avanti! ... Vamonos! – greetings and farewells
in several languages.

23/19 Well ... – in spite of the intervening *Pause*,
Carr's first line completes the limerick Joyce left
unfinished.

24/19 Stoical – versus 'Epicurean' means here,
roughly, self-denying versus self-indulgent (with
loose reference to opposed Ancient Greek
philosophies.)

– trenchfoot – gangrene from standing in flooded
trenches.

– hock – German sweet wine; 'seltzer' – fizzy
mineral water.

– post hock ... – 'post hoc, ergo propter hoc'
(Latin for 'if it's after that event, it was caused
by that event') is a philosophical assertion of
'causality' (tracing effects to causes) – which, as
Carr has already said on p. 10/8 and Tzara will
here confirm, was denied by Dada. Carr's pun
here is appalling, yet he means it: he reckons
the hock really does make him feel better.

– the war itself had causes – tracing 'causes' of
the First World War is a cliché task for
historians.

25/20 Narcissus – in myth, Narcissus fell in love with his own reflection.

27/21 sophistries – deceptive excuses.

– sit down and ... – the cliché is 'stand up and be counted'.

28/22 wog ... dago ... – racist abuse for anyone east of Dover.

– pedant – someone who fusses too much over the accuracy of individual 'phrases'.

– Frogs – French.

28/23 *Quite right!* – is savagely ironic; Tzara means 'quite wrong', and proceeds to offer a cynical historian's view of a 'cause of the First World War'.

29/23 We're here because ... – comes from a sad song of soldiers in the trenches.

blighty – originally Urdu, used in the British Raj to mean 'England': a wound which would get the soldier transferred safely back to England.

30/24 garrulity – talking too much.

– expose ... to comment – is an echo of *Earnest* (and so, distantly, is much of the next few pages, as far as p. 35/28).

32/35 discriminate mendacity – selective lying.

32/36 chaperone – a female escort for a young girl. 'Joyce' is a female first name. Joyce appears on p. 48/37 roughly in the role of Gwendolen's mother, Lady Bracknell.

– Homer's *Odyssey* ... Directory for 1904 – Joyce's novel follows characters through one day in Dublin in 1904, yet is based on episodes from Homer's poem. Writing *Ulysses* abroad, Joyce took pains to check the Dublin details.

- unusual combination – Stoppard has always delighted in unusual combinations which turn out to have natural explanations – see, for example, George's appearance on p. 32/45 of *Jumpers*.

34/27 'Vergleichen ...' – Gwen speaks the whole poem in English on p. 44/35.

- last word – alphabetically.

- Beethoven sonata – see p. 79.

35/28 decadent nihilists – degraded people who believe in nothing.

- CARR (*With great interest*) – the Wilde plot of the Victorian man's double-life (here Jack/ Tristan) is thus instantly linked to the twentieth-century 'spy' plot. Carr will pose as 'Tristan' to meet Cecily to learn Lenin's plans (as he was instructed to do on p. 18/15).

- 'Did you say the reference section?' roughly corresponds to Algernon writing the manor house's address on his shirt-cuff.

- the further left you go ... like their art – this has often been true.

- chit – note.

36/29 philistine – someone with no feeling for the arts.

37/29 expatriate – living abroad.

37/30 Dublin, don't tell me you know it? – was the final line of a limerick in their previous nonsense meeting on p. 20. Gwen's next speech begins another limerick (rhymes at 'rude', 'do', 'day' and 'say') but 'Do you know Mr Tzara, the poet?' completes not *this* rhyme scheme, but the previous one.

38/30   glaucoma – (a disease of the eyes) and 'inflation' refer back to 'sight and reputation'. As he goes on to say, Joyce did suffer severe eye problems; he is hinting that Tzara's reputation is inflated (excessively high).

  – monocular – in one eye only. Tzara 'affects' a monocle he may not need.

  – eyesore – Joyce may indeed be an ugly sight because of his muddled clothing.

  – expectorations – spittings (instead of 'expectations')

  – 'evacuate' – presumably instead of 'erect' (which might also have carried a double meaning).

39/31   ... no room for development – a line from *Earnest*. Doris (also p. 41/33 'Janice', p. 44/34 'Phyllis') expresses Carr's irritation at having been misled by the name 'Joyce' (p. 33/37).

40/31   wight – (chosen for alliteration) man. For a reference to this poem and Joyce's neutralism, see Stoppard's foreword, p. ix/xi.

40/32   shambles – slaughter-house.

  – I paid back my way – a nice reversal of a line in *Ulysses*: 'The proudest boast of an Englishman is: "I paid my way".'

41/33   raked – sloping ('totter' and 'alpine' suggest absurdly steep raking).

  – *Patience!* – Joyce takes it as advice, but Carr here and in his next speech is crying the names of Gilbert and Sullivan operettas.

     – Gomorrahist – Carr improvises this to avoid
saying 'sodomite' in Gwen's hearing – Sodom
and Gomorrah were twin cities of corruption
(Genesis 18). Gwen shows her opinion of this
evasion on p. 44/34, in the particularly apt
phrase 'Silly bugger'.

42/33 Goneril – ruthless female character in
Shakespeare's *King Lear*. In 1998 (to the
Financial Times) Stoppard recalled that 'in 1974
you felt you were collecting the whole of the
audience with that line. In 1993, you were
collecting about a quarter of the audience, and
three-quarters had no idea what she was talking
about.' Most of the 1974 audience would be
familiar with Shakespeare, and would also have
been to single-sex schools where plays were put
on by single-sex casts.

     – swell – dandy. Carr suddenly becomes
interested.

45/35 tear him for his bad verses ... mine for my –
love – every word in these lines is from
Shakespeare, a collage from sonnets and plays
including *Julius Caesar, Hamlet, As You Like
It, Much Ado About Nothing, Othello* and *I
Henry IV*. Sorting them could pass the time for
a Shakespeare fan confined to bed with a
temperature.

46/36 'Darling' ... – the embarrassing eroticism of the
cut-up sonnet is typical Stoppard: random
ingredients reassembled to make new sense.

     – Pray don't ... from here till 'semi-recumbent
posture' (p. 48/37) is a muddle of echoes of
Earnest.

48/37 Rise, sir ... – Lady Bracknell's line when re-entering the room in Act One of *Earnest*, after which she questions Jack on his eligibility as a husband.
cast in the form of the Christian Catechism – indeed the next two pages – as well as parodying Lady Bracknell's interrogation of Jack (see next note) – do follow the coldly scientific manner of the penultimate chapter of *Ulysses*, which itself imitates the Catechism (a series of doctrinal questions and answers).

– gardenia – a flower.

49/38 sacerdotal – like a priest.

49/39 in the public domain – able to be quoted at length in a book or on stage without the author's permission.

50/39 synchronously – simultaneously.

53/41 God send you don't ... – a joke (with 'pot' for 'hat' from the first chapter of *Ulysses*.

– cutting fancy figures at the wake – dancing at the funeral.

– baroque – here, intricately crafted.

– magician – adds significance to Joyce's conjuring act.

– capriciously – whimsically, without logic.

– contiguously – alongside.

54/42 I would strongly advise you ... – Lady Bracknell's grilling of Jack nears its close with 'I would strongly advise you, Mr Worthing, to try and acquire some relations ... before the season is quite over.'

– 'Really, if ...' – Carr is now learning his part in

146

Wilde's play. These lines will be repeated by Lenin on p. 74/58.

Act Two

58/46 *his manner betrays this* – Carr needs to be a recognisable cartoon spy at this point if the audience is to remember the 'spy' plot. A reminder: In Wilde's Act Two, Algernon plays 'Ernest' in order to meet Cecily; here Carr (who played Algernon in Joyce's production) is playing 'Tristan' in order to meet Cecily in order to learn Lenin's plans.

59/47 ruminate – think: this adaptation of 'urinate' (p. 52/41) is even more surreal; it also suggests that Cecily may have been given a censored version.

– louche and devil-take-the-hindmost – devious and reckless.

– voluptuous – highly sensual; 'disdain' – i.e., for morality.

– I don't think you ought ... – the coy words of Wilde's Cecily to Algernon; here brilliantly revived on pp. 64/50 and 66/52.

60/47 Any kind at all – Carr is not a very practised spy!

– a sympathetic chord – see p. 31/25: Cecily is exploring poetry on the same alphabetical principle.

60/48 references – Carr takes this to mean 'recommendations for a departing employee'. So inept is he as a spy (and so distracted by Cecily, perhaps) that he has temporarily forgotten the name of his target. In his next speech he belatedly (and rather transparently) addresses his task.

61/48 trying to ingratiate themselves – in the most ancient of comic traditions, Cecily is inadvertently referring to Carr and herself.

   – (*ashamed*) – since Switzerland has no border anywhere near a sea, the instructions confirm British incompetence.

   – Break a leg – traditional ironic message wishing actors good luck.

   – Horace – Horace Rumbold was the British Minister in Berne, Switzerland; he was fiercely travestied by Joyce in *Ulysses*.

62/49 I have a servant myself – the ancient tradition again: Carr's servant is the very one being discussed. In the next three lines: Cecily, as Lenin's disciple, disapproves of *employing* servants. She sees a future where no one will be allowed to do so, but Carr takes her to mean that under socialism no one will have 'scruples'.

63/49 Ars longa, vita brevis – art is long-lasting, life is brief. But Cecily (who now seems only too well-informed) thinks she heard a reference to Wilde's homosexual 'proclivities' (tendencies). This innuendo replaces 1974 jokes potentially offensive to Irishmen (Wilde was Irish by birth).

   – to boot – 'in addition'; but obvious puns follow.

   – uncommitted – i.e., politically. The line is of course an adaptation of Joyce's line on p. 42/33, which itself echoed *Earnest*.

63/50 Gilbert but not ... – compare 'I know him, but not her.'

64/50 if you knew – adapted from a popular song, 'If You Knew Susie'. Carr then hurls out the titles of Gilbert and Sullivan operettas in the fierceness of his devotion to them; but it sounds like the fierceness of swearing (a joke borrowed from Beckett's *Waiting for Godot*).

– Here is an article – at this point Cecily gives Carr the folder which she picked up by mistake on p. 3/3 – actually a chapter of *Ulysses*.

64/51 my work – on the contrary, his work as Consul made such interest essential.

65/51 Ramsay MacDonald – British Prime Minister in 1924 and 1929–35.

– 'Flora Macdonald' saved the life of ('Bonnie') Prince Charles Edward after the battle of Culloden in 1746.

– Bolshie – from Bolshevik, ignorant slang between the wars for any socialist or even any rebel. The next joke is that Carr suddenly becomes far from ignorant, giving us an entirely 'straight' summary of how 'Marx got it wrong'. He forgets he is a spy and heatedly tries to change Cecily's views; he may also appear to stop being Carr, and to speak directly for Tom Stoppard. All is perhaps excusable in a travesty, and in Carr's final sentence ('How sweet...') the toy train gets back on the rails of the notional plot.

– *Das Kapital* – Marx's major work.

66/52 Kant – a leading rationalist philosopher, but there is a bawdy pun.

- The only way ... – above (this book, p. 128), I regret Stoppard's revision of this speech. Theatrically, however, much of its brilliance survives. The stripper act remains refreshing and funny; Carr is seen to be reassuringly human, and this literary travesty nicely reverses the unfaltering smoothness of Wilde's Algernon, who seems never disturbed by anything so crude as lust. The point is confirmed when the lights 'snap back' from Carr's frenzied 'Get 'em off!' to a conversation of Wildean urbanity.

67/53 Oh, Cecily! – it is Cecily who drags Carr out of sight; and the fact that he has his jacket off by the bottom of the page suggests that he is prospering in the encounter. But ironically her action also enables him to carry out his duty as spy (which is why we see him pop up).

- Chasuble and Prism – discussed above, this book, p. 127.

70/54 'and that I hope ... – in Wilde the words are 'and that I intend to lead a better life in the future'. The revised words refer to Carr's 'moral dilemma' (see next page).

71/55 ... that I might share with you and Mr Tzara? – see p. 62/49. This is savagely sarcastic, but neither Bennett nor Tzara shows a flicker of embarrassment.

71/56 shocked ... so-called duty – a Wildean reversal. Carr is thinking of acting patriotically (revealing Lenin's plans) at the cost of his love for Cecily. It is also obviously Wildean that this 'moral dilemma' must wait till the muffins are finished.

150

72/56 dialectic – Marxist jargon; here, the historical struggle between different views which will eventually result in world Communism.

– If Lenin did not exist ... invent him – a travesty-reversal of the eighteenth-century French writer Voltaire's line: 'If God did not exist, it would be necessary to invent him.'

73/57 micturition – urination.

– I don't think ... for us in it! – Carr foresees (rightly) that Modernist movements such as Dada will be suppressed by the Communists. Tzara appears on the other hand to mean 'a place for us' as 'a need for us'.

– No, it is perfectly clear in my mind – but in the 1993 sequence he makes the opposite decision; see note to p. 74/58.

74/58 Really, if ... moral responsibility! – discussed above, this book pp. 127–8.

– another man might have cracked – this is a cliché from spy or war fiction; the usual context would be pressure to give up knowledge, and perhaps betray one's country. The reversal here is that if Carr *had* cracked (by revealing Lenin's plans to the British authorities) he would have been betraying his 'feelings for Cecily' and thus 'stopped the whole Bolshevik thing'. In the 1974 original, this speech came on what would be p. 70/55 of our present text, three pages *before* the 'decisively' speech which now (p. 73/57) precedes it. Thus in the original it seemed that Carr eventually *did* resolve to tell the British – though only (as here on p. 73/57) when it was probably too late, Lenin's train having already left. Stoppard's awareness that changing the position of this speech must also change its emphasis is clear from the fact that he also added a new and reinforcing phrase: 'the future of the civilised world'.

76/60   Bosh ... affectation – Carr's voice, chiming with Lenin's, is a 1993 addition. Since they represent utterly opposed but equally blinkered ideologies, their shared dismissal of art speaks as strongly in its favour as Joyce in Act One. Carr's speech about Mayakovsky and Tzara is also new in 1993.

80/62   'Mr Gallagher and Mr Shean' – an American music-hall song from the 1920s. The whole song presents a travesty-version of the justly-famous encounter of Cecily and Gwendolen over tea, the climax of the second act of Earnest.

82/64   tête-à-tête – in modern idiom, a one-to-one.

83/65   hanging up his hat – giving up everything (for the cause of the common people, the 'proletariat').

   –   stream of consciousness – a technique developed in Ulysses, and incidentally travestied by Stoppard in Old Carr's speeches on pp. 6–11/5–11.

84/66   Is it done ... – is it socially approved of? Gwendolen implies that Cecily is just out to hook any man. In Earnest the emphasis is the other way: 'CECILY: No doubt you have many other calls of a similar character to make in the neighbourhood.'

- au fait – French for 'up to date'; pronounced 'oh fay'.

85/66 luminary – a leading light. Adapted quotations from *Earnest* follow.

85/67 Very ... well ... – see pp. 3/3 and 64/50. Carr has been reading Joyce's draft, as if it were a 'social critique'; Tzara has been reading Lenin's as if it were 'art for art's sake'. They are 'hypocrites' in having momentarily pretended (to pacify their girlfriends) to admire what they have read.

87/67 Sofia – capital of Bulgaria; but Tzara comes from Romania, which, contrary to Carr's Consular impression, is *not* the same place.

87/68 Perrier-Jouet, Brut, '89 – the wine to which Algernon helped himself in *Earnest*. But this time Bennett has taken it, and the social revolution is well under way.

88/68 Quadri-oculate – four-eyed (reference to Joyce's spectacles).

89/69 where is the missing chapter??? – in *Earnest*, Lady Bracknell thunders: 'Prism! Where is that baby?'

90/70 connected with midwifery – that the Joyce chapter is indeed connected links neatly to Wilde's plot of the missing infant.

- yes, I said yes ... – comes from the final page of *Ulysses*.

92/71 (BLACKOUT.) – Craig Werner (*Arizona Quarterly*, 1979) describes the curtain call of the New York production: 'Throughout the play actor John Wood made the transition from the role of Old Carr to that of Young Carr by removing his old bathrobe and altering his carriage. Following the play, Wood hobbles out wearing the bathrobe, bows and removes the bathrobe, only to reveal another bathrobe, and another Old Carr, underneath.'

Arcadia

Arcadia was first performed in 1993, to general acclaim. Of all this dramatist's works it has the strongest story-line and the largest cast of convincing characters: it also engages most subtly and yet accessibly with a wide range of intellectual material. Stoppard here abandons his old cartoon mode in favour of relative realism, though much enhanced and teased about by the alternation of two eras, which then, in a great ultimate scene, take the stage together. A few years after its first performance, *Arcadia* seems the Stoppard play (along perhaps with *Rosencrantz*) least likely to date, most likely to deserve future revivals.

The play brings together in one room two periods, 1809–12 and the present. Not surprisingly, it is about change, in fashion and in knowledge; yet also about two unchanging facts of human life: sexual attraction and death.

The setting is Sidley Park, a very large English country house owned and occupied both Then and Now by the same aristocratic family, the Coverlys, the head of which always holds the title of Lord Croom. The house and its park were designed to form a perfect country environment, like the imaginary 'Arcadia' of the Latin poet Virgil, where idealised shepherds and shepherdesses conducted their affairs. But reference is made several times to a Latin line, 'Et in Arcadia ego', which is famously ambiguous. At first glance the words can seem cheerful enough: 'I too am in Arcadia'. But the most well-known occurrence of the line is in a painting by Nicolas Poussin of 1638–9 (now in the Louvre), where it forms the inscription on a tomb, puzzled over by Arcadian shepherds. Are these the imagined words of the person within the tomb? – 'I too lived in Arcadia once'? Or, since an alternative meaning of 'et' is 'even', are the words spoken by Death itself? 'Even in Arcadia, I am here'. This last grim interpretation is the one presented in Stoppard's play, where death intrudes on the privileged setting, taking two gifted young lives.

The play also shows how human notions of an ideal environment, an Arcadia, keep changing. In 1730, the gardens of Sidley Park were geometrical in an Italian style; by 1760 they had been replaced by sweeping vistas, a would-be 'natural' landscape associated with eighteenth-century **Enlightenment**; and when the play opens, in 1809, this is all to be altered again into a 'Gothic' style with artificial crags, ruins and hermitage. In 1809 the Enlightenment is yielding to **Romanticism**, in what the historical writer Hannah describes (p. 37) as 'the decline from thinking to feeling'. At the same time in physics a few holes were beginning to appear in the elegant, balancing patterns discovered by Newton; and in *Arcadia* the teenage Thomasina, keen on the new Gothic fashion in gardening, longs for science to reach beyond regularity. With the fresh vision of a genius, she insists there must be an equation for a bluebell.

In the second period, the Now, the old gardens are being researched by the wife of the present owner, while Hannah and a literature academic, Bernard, are researching past events in the house, particularly those involving one guest who became famous, Lord Byron. The heir to the house, Valentine, is a scientist; he discovers Thomasina's notebooks and recognises her inspired hunches towards what are now called chaos theory and thermodynamics. These notions – randomness, and the gradual running-down of the world – were of their time, 'Gothic', in departing from Enlightenment theory, but otherwise impossibly ahead of their time: they are modern knowledge, which Thomasina had neither the mathematics nor the computers to develop. Her fate and that of her tutor Septimus bring darkness to the play; but her present-day relative Valentine talks of chaos theory with an exhilaration which may be shared by Stoppard, since it echoes so much in his earlier work:

> The unpredictable and the predetermined unfold together to make everything the way it is. It's how nature creates itself, on every scale, the snowflake and the snowstorm. It makes me so happy ... It's the best possible time to be alive, when almost everything you thought you knew is wrong. (p. 63)

An alternative explanation for unpredictability is offered by Valentine's eighteen-year-old sister Chloe: the apparently chance nature of sexual attraction.

> The universe is deterministic all right, just like Newton said, I mean it's trying to be, but the only thing going wrong is people fancying people who aren't supposed to be in the plan. (p. 97)

The first words of *Arcadia* are about sex, and most of its characters turn out to be in love – but unluckily: their beloveds don't respond and/or are of the 'wrong' age or social position. Blind Cupid fires his darts of love at random. For all the pain this brings, it is the stuff of comedy, which is about the muddles and misfits of our lives, the gaps between the ideal and the reality. Stoppard, whose previous work was sometimes seen as 'all head and no heart', here beautifully intertwines intellectual puzzlement with the frustrations of, as Valentine puts it, 'the attraction Newton left out'. At the same time he focuses on a particular moment at which a faith in Enlightenment – the predictability of everything by rational method – was challenged and began to crumble; and on a particular historical figure in whom many of these oppositions seem to come together. That figure remains always teasingly just offstage, typically riding away at four a.m. after a married woman is found on the threshold of his bedroom: George Gordon, Lord Byron.

Synopsis

Act One

SCENE ONE 1809. Lady Thomasina, aged thirteen, has heard the butler, Jellaby, telling the cook that Mr Noakes the landscape architect has seen through his spy-glass Mrs Chater in the gazebo, in 'carnal embrace'; she asks her tutor Septimus what the words mean. Septimus is at this moment trying to read a poem by Mrs Chater's husband; he senses danger, gives Thomasina an absurd answer and attempts to distract her with the unproved last theorem of the seventeenth-century mathematician Fermat. When she presses him, however, he does give her an accurate clinical summary of the sexual act.

On p. 5, Jellaby delivers to Septimus a letter from Chater which demands an answer; he replies with a calm acceptance. To Thomasina he describes Noakes as the 'serpent' in Sidley Park. But she is more interested in the irreversibility of jam in her rice pudding. A moment later she is thinking about determinism: if Newton is right then it should theoretically be possible to foresee every future event. This surprises Septimus; he draws her back (p. 7) to Fermat, who announced his proof in a marginal note where there was no space to write it out. She decides it was just a 'joke' by Fermat, to make future generations of mathematicians mad. She is dismissed when Chater bursts in (p. 8).

Septimus is not at all cowed by Chater. He neither denies his encounter with Mrs Chater nor apologises; instead he distracts Chater by grotesquely over-praising his poetry. The Chaters are at Sidley Park as the guests of Lady Croom's brother, Captain Brice, whose own name has been linked in gossip with Mrs Chater's.

Chater is wholly won over by Septimus's false praise, and is affectionately (though ineptly) inscribing his copy when Noakes enters, dismayed to find the two men on the best of terms. Lady Croom and Captain Brice arrive, naming parts of the grounds which Noakes proposes to ruin – but Septimus and Chater believe they are naming places where Septimus and Mrs Chater are supposed to have met. Thomasina sorts out this confusion (p. 14) but instantly starts another one by saying that her tutor has taught her 'everything' about 'carnal embrace'.

Noakes has been employed by Lord Croom, against his wife's wishes; she fears he will spoil Sidley Park, which at present is 'nature as God intended' (p. 16). She quotes the inscription 'Et in Arcadia ego' and translates it as 'Here I am in Arcadia'. On p. 17 sounds are heard of a shooting-party, which includes a friend of Septimus. Tutor and pupil are left onstage, and the guns' 'slaughter' provokes

Septimus's different translation of the Latin: 'even in Arcadia, there am I', 'I' being Death. Thomasina understands his meaning but briskly dismisses such gloomy talk. On Noakes's sketch of a projected hermitage, she draws in an imaginary hermit, and as she does so casually asks Septimus, 'Are you in love with my mother?' He avoids replying; she gives him a note from Mrs Chater.

SCENE TWO Page 19; present-day. Hannah is seen looking through Noakes's sketch book; then leaves. Chloe Coverly, eighteen, enters with Bernard, and reveals that the Miss Jarvis he is due to meet is Hannah Jarvis, the best-selling author. Bernard hastily asks her not to tell Hannah his real surname. Chloe leaves; her fifteen-year-old brother Gus is glimpsed and her older brother, Valentine, keeps coming and going. Finally Bernard speaks to Valentine and learns that the room, which has seemed like a passageway, will be just that tonight, cleared of much of its furniture because of a public dance.

Bernard, an academic doing literary research, phoned Valentine yesterday (having failed to get a reply from Lord Croom) and was told to come today and talk with Hannah, who is staying in the house with Lady Croom's blessing in order to research the Sidley Park hermit. Valentine reveals that he works with computers. When Hannah arrives (top of p. 26) Bernard prattles at her, unconvincingly praising her book on Lady Caroline Lamb. He claims (p. 28) he is here to research the poet Chater. Hannah reveals that she dislikes academics because they review her books harshly; (p. 30) that she and Valentine have a 'joke' that she is his fiancée; and that the present Lady Croom is also doing research, into the past gardens of the Park. On p. 33, they study

Thomasina's p. 18 sketch of an imaginary hermit, mistaking it for an actual portrait, and Noakes and the 'picturesque' movement are described. The hermit, we are told (p. 36), was 'suspected of genius', filling his cottage with sheets of 'proofs that the world was coming to an end'. The change in landscape gardening represented the change from the Enlightenment to Romanticism, 'from thinking to feeling'.

Bernard appears more interested in Byron than Chater, and on p. 39 Chloe blurts out his real surname (which he has concealed because he wrote a scathing review of Hannah's last book). Hannah is furious but Bernard wants them to co-operate. He produces Chater's book, a copy which was sold as Byron's but which contains the letters we have seen Septimus receive. Byron left England in 1809; Bernard now believes (p. 42) this was because he had killed Chater in a duel over Chater's wife. On p. 43 they realise that Septimus and Byron were together at school and university.

Delighted, Bernard kisses Hannah – as Chloe enters. He leaves; Chloe, noting 'sexual energy' in him, thinks of inviting him to the dance as Hannah's partner. She also says that her 'brother' is in love with Hannah – who takes this to mean Valentine, but a moment later (p. 45) understands that it refers to Gus, as he silently presents her with an apple.

SCENE THREE We are back in 1809, and again with tutor and pupil. Septimus has received another 'internal' letter via the butler, and is now writing one 'for the post'. His friend and house-guest referred to on p. 17 is Lord Byron. Thomasina describes her own mother flirting with him (p. 48), and also Byron laughing (in Chater's presence) in recollection of Septimus's dismissive review of Chater's first book.

In her work, Thomasina is getting ahead. She finds ordinary geometry too regular and limited – there must somewhere be an equation for a bluebell (p. 49). When Septimus says such equations are for God, she calls him a 'faint-heart'.

Cleopatra (subject of the Latin she is translating) makes Thomasina grieve for the knowledge lost by fire in ancient Egypt (p. 50), but Septimus is more philosophical: 'Mathematical discoveries glimpsed and lost to view will have their time again.' (The page has grim dramatic irony because Thomasina will die in a fire and Septimus will go mad trying to deal with her mathematics.) But when Septimus pretends that Shakespeare's version of the Cleopatra passage is his own, Thomasina rushes out 'in tears of rage' (p. 52).

Chater arrives, for another showdown with Septimus, this time supported by Captain Brice. Septimus remains unruffled, and they are interrupted by Lady Croom, excited over Byron. She asks Septimus to persuade him to stay, but also to take over his pistols (at which Chater goggles). Septimus (p. 55) contrives to insult Brice too, and arranges to duel with Chater at 5 a.m. and Brice at 5.05; he calmly implies he will kill them both and will have to leave the country, after which, he suggests, Byron might remain to tutor Thomasina.

SCENE FOUR Present-day. Hannah reads to Valentine words written by Thomasina in her maths primer, claiming to have discovered 'the New Geometry of Irregular Forms'. In the next room Gus is improvising on the piano. Valentine sees that Thomasina was attempting to use with pencil and paper the technique he uses on a computer, of iterated algorithms. He outlines changes in modern mathematics (p. 58), his own work on grouse (p. 60), and chaos theory (p. 63). He uses the metaphor of trying to hear a tune in jumbled piano music, and compares Thomasina's efforts to doodling at a piano.

Hannah talks about Gus. He is seen by his mother as a genius, having corrected at 'first go' an excavation for a former boat-house.

Bernard enters (p. 64). In a copy of Byron's poems he has found pencilled lines abusing Chater; and also a letter showing that by 1810 Chater was dead and Mrs Chater had married Captain Brice. Valentine says that a game book confirms that Byron did stay here. Bernard rushes out to find it. Valentine says (p. 67) that Lady Croom is 'in a flutter about Bernard'.

Hannah asks why no one did algorithms in the past: Valentine said that before computers it would have taken impossibly long and mountains of paper: 'you'd have to be insane'. Hannah realised this sounds like her hermit. Gus drags his brother off to the dressing-up box, to find costumes for tonight's dance.

The act closes with a change to early morning light, and the sound of a distant pistol shot.

Act Two

SCENE FIVE Page 70; present-day. To Chloe, Valentine and Hannah, Bernard reads aloud his draft lecture claiming that Byron shot Chater in a duel over Mrs Chater. He over-rides their doubts, though Hannah warns him he may make a public fool of himself (p. 78). He is rude about her work, Valentine dismisses all work about 'personalities' (p. 80) and Bernard defends poetry. He upsets both Valentine and Chloe, who leave. He tells Hannah she had 'the wrong bloke' on the jacket of her latest book; then suddenly invites her to accompany him to London 'for sex'. She declines, and it emerges (p. 85) that he has been having sex with Chloe.

Bernard has found a reference to the hermit owning a pet tortoise. His taxi comes, and he leaves for London. Hannah shows Valentine a letter which describes the hermit (p. 87) as mad from pursuing a French mathematical theory that the world was running down. Valentine diagnoses this as the second law of thermodynamics, unknown in Septimus's time. Hannah spots that Septimus was born in the same year as the hermit, and is now convinced they were the same man.

SCENE SIX The same early light and pistol shot that ended Act One; but this is 1809. Jellaby admits Septimus, who carries two pistols: for a moment we assume he has killed Chater (and perhaps Brice too) – then he produces a dead rabbit. He slept the night in the boat-house, anticipating the duel.

Septimus extracts from Jellaby a cautiously worded account of the night's events: Lady Croom 'encountered' Mrs Chater on the threshold of Byron's room, and later 'looked for' Septimus in his. She then sent Brice and the Chaters packing, and Byron also left, without returning Septimus's copy of Chater's poem.

Lady Croom herself enters (p. 90). In Septimus's room she found and read two letters from him, though they were marked to be opened only 'in the event of my death'. One was a love-letter to herself; the other was to Thomasina, about rice pudding. She also claims (p. 92) that Mrs Chater was 'discovered in Lord Byron's room' by Mr Chater; but Septimus has already heard otherwise. While apologising for having introduced Byron 'to your notice', Septimus in fact threatens Lady Croom herself – he can always ask Byron for the full story.

Jellaby brings a letter left by Byron for Septimus, who declares that he too will leave Sidley Park, and in front of Lady Croom burns the letter unread. We now learn that the Chaters and Brice are all sailing together to the West Indies. Lady Croom expresses surprise at Septimus's writing a love-letter to her so soon after sex with Mrs Chater; he ingeniously claims to have been imagining Lady Croom all the time. She makes an assignation for him to visit her in the evening.

SCENE SEVEN Present-day. Valentine and Chloe are in Regency dress, and Gus is choosing similar clothes for himself. Bernard's lecture has been publicised in newspapers. Chloe produces her own explanation for the victory of chaos over determinism – people falling in love with the wrong others.

Left alone with Hannah, Valentine tries again to flirt with her, then gets on with his computer iterations, which Hannah (p. 100) finds beautiful. They are Thomasina's equations. Hannah reveals that she burned to death on the night before her seventeenth birthday.

From page 102 till the end of the play, 1812 and present-day share the stage. While Hannah and Valentine work quietly at their researches, the people they are researching enter: Augustus chases Thomasina in, and stays for her drawing lesson with Septimus. Valentine continues to explain to Hannah the second law of thermodynamics.

Byron is now famous. Thomasina persuades herself that three years ago he and she 'exchanged significant glances'. Her brother remembers Byron claiming a hare actually shot by himself. On p. 107 we learned why he is so smug this morning – Thomasina has told him that Septimus kissed her in the newly built hermitage. But apparently this merely sealed Septimus's promise to teach her to waltz.

Septimus is reading a report of scientific discoveries in Paris, which he passes to Thomasina. The piano is being played by Count Zelinsky, with whom we are told Lady Croom is in love. The steam pump is heard. Lady Croom enters and watches Thomasina reading.

Chloe enters (p. 109), trying to assemble everyone in Regency dress for a photograph. Lady Croom grumbles about the steam pump, Septimus about Zelinsky's music. We learn that flowers on the table are dahlias discovered by Chater in Martinique, that he died there soon after-wards, and that Mrs Chater promptly married Captain Brice. Hannah simultaneously discovers the same infor-mation in a garden book, and leaves to tell Bernard he has made a fool of himself.

Thomasina is excited by the Parisian essay. Is it geometry? asks her mother; Thomasina dismisses that idea, but we do incidentally learn that she has not abandoned her hopes of discovering the geometry of irregular forms. Lady Croom decides she is becoming over-educated and needs to be married off. Cheekily, Thomasina then mentions Byron – whom Lady Croom and Septimus saw with Lady Caroline Lamb at the Royal Academy (so Hannah was right and Bernard wrong on p. 82–3).

Noakes enters (p. 113), to hear the wrath of Lady Croom. She asks whether he is going to supply a hermit for the hermitage; Septimus suggests it should be Zelinsky.

Thomasina tells Noakes his pump will always deliver less power than is put into it; we realise (p. 117) that she is now clearly ahead of Septimus. She leaves giving him her drawing of him with Plautus the tortoise.

Augustus enters, more subdued. He probably has some real respect for Septimus, and at least needs his help at this moment. Perhaps as a peace offering, he asks to be allowed to keep Thomasina's drawing – so it survives, in Augustus Lord Croom's library. Awkwardly, he then asks Septimus for information about sex (so another character is aware of 'the attraction that Newton left out'). They leave together. Bernard enters (p. 118), furious at what Hannah has found out; she says she will expose his error publicly. Chloe dresses Bernard in Regency clothes; he is aghast to hear that a photograph will be taken for the local press, yet is compelled to appear, whereas Hannah mysteriously escapes. The stage empties (p. 122), and the lights change to evening.

Septimus enters and starts reading Thomasina's work. She joins him, in her nightdress and secretive in manner. She kisses him and demands her waltz lesson. He is looking at her old primer and at what she wrote in the margin; she now dismisses it as a 'joke', which is what she also said (p. 8) about Fermat's marginal note. Septimus says it may nevertheless make him mad, and continues to read.

Hannah enters – also now (like the entire cast) in Regency dress. Valentine enters, half drunk, and (p. 125) expounds Thomasina's heat-exchange diagram to Hannah while Septimus also studies it. She had the right vision, though not the maths to prove it.

Septimus and Thomasina begin to waltz. Bernard enters and starts changing back into modern dress. Septimus and Thomasina embrace. Chloe bursts in; her mother caught her with Bernard in the hermitage. Bernard is leaving at once (p. 127), and refuses to take Chloe with him. He wishes Hannah well with her book; she says she knows who the hermit was but is missing the proof. She remains on stage, the only modern character.

Gus enters and watches her; the audience may think he is Augustus watching Septimus and Thomasina, as the tutor advises the pupil to be careful with her candle flame. She asks him three times to join her; three times he refuses. She decides to stay and dance more.

Gus gives Hannah Thomasina's drawing, captioned 'Septimus holding Plautus'. Since the hermit's tortoise is historically identified by this name (p. 85) this is the proof Hannah needed. Silently, Gus invites her to dance, and they do so 'rather awkwardly', as Septimus and Thomasina continue 'fluently'.

Classical and Romantic: Order and Disorder

By 1809 many political and intellectual shifts were occurring in England, but at the start of Stoppard's play they have scarcely penetrated rural Derbyshire. The education Thomasina is receiving from Septimus is that of the mid-eighteenth-century Enlightenment, also known as the Age of Reason: its regular forms and neatly fitting beliefs are sometimes described as 'Classical'. Her question (p. 6), 'Is God a Newtonian?' is not quite just a joke: it sums up the impression that the science of Isaac Newton (1642–1727) has potentially sorted out the universe, the rules by which the Divine Creator worked. In the Enlightenment, everything might eventually prove capable of explanation, within a rational God-given order. This unifying religious confidence is summed up in the poem of Joseph Addison (1672–1729), 'The spacious firmament on high', where sky, sun, moon and all the stars and planets

> ... spread the truth from pole to pole ...
> In reason's ear they all rejoice ...
> 'The hand that made us is divine.'

As it happens, a moment earlier Thomasina has noticed a small hole in Newton's physics, which will be steadily widened as the play continues: she can't unstir the jam from her rice pudding. And in a later scene (p. 49) she complains that the geometry she has been taught confines itself to simple shapes: she wants to move on to tackle those which seem random and irregular, such as that of a leaf. Her modern relative, Valentine, believes that randomness, disorder – or 'chaos' – is as much a part of reality as order, and that far from being infinitely reversible, as Newtonian physics suggested, the system is gradually running down: the jam indeed can't be unstirred. These ideas are further discussed in this book pp. 175–7.

In maths and physics Thomasina's intuitions are ahead of their time; but in other fields of life beyond Sidley Park changes are already advanced. Political revolution is in the air, and in music and literature old forms are being broken up and superseded. Today we think of 1809 as a year in which the Romantic movement was at its height, and one of the figures associated with it, Lord Byron, is actually staying at Sidley Park as Thomasina asks her question. Romanticism challenges the assumptions of Classicism or the Enlightenment and often deliberately reverses them, seeking out gloom and shadow, pursuing irrationality (dreams, visions, madness, drugs), and preferring wild, irregular landscapes untouched by civilisation.

Hannah makes her opinion of this very clear, on p. 36:

> The whole Romantic sham, Bernard! It's what happened to the Enlightenment, isn't it? A century of intellectual rigour turned in on itself ... In a setting of cheap thrills and false emotion ... The decline from thinking to feeling.

But Hannah copes with life by trying to deny feeling; and a more balanced view accepts Romanticism as a further development in human understanding. By making Thomasina want to investigate irregular forms, Stoppard establishes a vague parallel between Romanticism and modern chaos theory – seeing the latter as a sort of Romantic maths. (The analogy is developed by Valentine on p. 59).

An early, popular manifestation of Romanticism, or at least of reaction against the Enlightenment, was the cult of the 'Gothic', the thrillingly wild, medieval and grotesque. This developed through the eighteenth century, almost as a kind of counter-culture, in painting, literature – and in garden design.

The Symbolism of Gardens

In religion and myth, gardens often appear as places of perfection, where the potentially chaotic forces of Nature have been tamed and ordered by the gods. And myths of course reflect human dreams; even in cities, even on the rooftop of a tower block, a garden made where we live is a version of Nature as we prefer to see it.

The ornamental gardens or *parterres* made for large country houses in the late seventeenth century are now relatively rare in Britain, though surviving more frequently on the European continent. They allow Nature in only cautiously, caged by tight symmetry and plenty of clipping. The human hand must be visibly in control, the difference between garden and wilderness emphasised; islands of achieved rationality must be kept separate from a still alarming universe. Hannah, on p. 36, sees Sidley Park in 1730 as 'Paradise in the age of reason ... topiary, pools and terraces, fountains, an avenue of limes ... sublime geometry'.

By the mid-eighteenth century the great country houses have become less uneasy about their relationship to Nature. The landscape around them is still designed, most famously by Capability Brown (p. 36 again), but is now intended to look 'natural' – though such schemes are still carefully selective, excluding brambles and swamp in favour of sheep-grazed greensward and pretty lakes that will not flood, or, as Hannah on p. 34 puts it, 'open water, clumps of trees, classical boat-house'. She traces this fashion to a painterly-literary ideal (Claude–Virgil–Arcadia); but its *apparent* naturalness also reflects the confidence of the Enlightenment: since Nature is all laid out by God, the grounds of a great house should appear to embrace rather than resist it. This is the thinking behind the Sidley Park which Lady Croom describes (the irony is Stoppard's more than hers) as 'the right amount of sheep ... tastefully arranged ... Nature as God intended' (p. 16).

But no sooner is something fashionable than its replacement is evolving. The emphasis on God's super-vision of Nature led to curiosity about things which were natural yet not civilised. Even in the early eighteenth century the metropolitan poet Alexander Pope installed a 'grotto', an artificial cavern, in his garden. Between 1739 and 1741 Horace Walpole toured Europe and returned with ideas of the 'picturesque' which had more to do with wildness than civilisation. Back home, he built a 'Gothic' garden, and in 1764 published what has been called 'the prototype Gothic novel', *The Castle of Otranto* (see p. 17). In 1773 the exemplary figure of London coffee-houses, Dr Samuel Johnson, made the astonishing decision to tour the more remote regions of Scotland – wild indeed in those days. Thus even as the average person was coming to terms with Enlightenment, others were instinctively moving beyond it. In the following fifty or more years, 'wild' became a buzz-word.

'Gothic' implied things medieval, a reversion back beyond the earlier 'enlightenment' of the Renaissance. The Gothic revival involved what we might nowadays call 'virtual reality'; its consumers could be thrilled by the mystery and primitive violence of an earlier age without actually suffering its risks or inconveniences. Thus, as is well mocked in Jane Austen's *Northanger Abbey*, the reader of Gothic romances went safely to sleep in a modern bed. Though travellers such as Johnson endured genuine discomfort in the wild, the garden designs of Sir Humphry Repton (1752–1818) – see p. 13 – were thoroughly synthetic, manufacturing 'ruins', 'crags' and 'hermitages' as if for a modern theme park. Such notions of the picturesque derived partly from paintings of Salvator Rosa (1615–73), summed up by the mid-eighteenth-century poet James Thomson as 'savage Rosa' (the adjective by this time expressing relish), and eventually reaching Derbyshire and the thirteen-year-old Thomasina in 1809, when they seem to her brilliantly fashionable. As a fad in gardening, then, Noakes's changes represent the deliberate importation of pretend-wildness. He can supply a hermitage, but when asked

(p. 115) to supply a hermit he can only suggest advertising in the press. This is Stoppard bordering on his old cartoon mode, but Lady Croom makes the ironic point well: 'a hermit who takes a newspaper is not a hermit in whom one can have complete confidence'.

Byron

It is hard to guess what kind of Arcadia might have been designed by the real-life person behind this fictional play: Byron (1788–1824) is a highly ambivalent figure, part conservative and part radical. 'Lord Byron' was his inherited title; born an aristocrat, he might have been expected to hold conservative views; and his literary loyalties were backward-looking, to classical and eighteenth-century satire, while he was highly scornful of the pioneer Romantic poets Wordsworth and Coleridge. On the other hand, his own early success was in more-or-less Gothic melodrama – 'Childe Harold's Pilgrimage, A Romaunt', which Thomasina rapturously describes on p. 105 as 'poetical and pathetic'. In 1811 it brought Byron instant fame and he became in popular eyes the rebel hero of his own life – seen by Lady Croom 'everywhere' in London, 'posing' (p. 113), with the underclad Lady Caroline Lamb on his arm. A series of sexual scandals drove him permanently abroad, where he became active in revolutionary causes and eventually died of fever. After his death the image of the pouting 'Byronic' hero became more influential than ever on the European continent.

Thus Byron is traditionally known as a sort of ultra-Romantic, who placed himself beyond civilised society by his sexual promiscuity, which probably included a brief incestuous affair with his half-sister. Yet his manner was that of the Regency beau (such as Beau Brummel – p. 45) and modern critics feel (as he did himself) that his best writing is as a social satirist, ironic rather than revolutionary. He contained within himself some of the tensions examined in *Arcadia*: classical v. Romantic, order v. randomness, rationality v. sexual impulse. And he hovers repeatedly behind the play, though Stoppard wisely resists the temptation to allow him on stage. Just as *Rosencrantz* happens in the wings of *Hamlet*, so *Arcadia* is situated in imaginary footnotes to Byron's life – footnotes which indeed Bernard Nightingale is determined to write.

Byron is the subject of Bernard's career dreams, and the part-subject of Hannah's achieved success – her bestseller about Lady Caroline Lamb. Back in 1809, Thomasina notes her mother falling in love with him; and in 1812, when he has become famous, fantasises about marrying him herself. He causes havoc in the small hours at Sidley Park; like his own Don Juan, he demonstrates at its most unruly the 'chaos' caused by sex, by what Chloe calls (p. 97) 'people fancying people who aren't supposed to be in that part of the plan'.

Determinism, Free Will, and the Apple in the Garden

Determinism declares that future events are predetermined. The faith behind this may be in a dictatorial God, unwilling to leave any aspect of his Creation to chance; or in 'laws' of physical science (see Thomasina on p. 7); or in, say, Marxist theory (see *Travesties*) or modern genetics. The common element is the belief that human beings have little or no freedom of decision, even when they think they have.

Free will is obviously the opposite concept. Individuals are able to make choices affecting their actions and their lives. The Judaeo-Christian idea is that although God is omnipotent, he decided not to predetermine everything for humankind. He wanted us to *choose* to be good.

In Genesis, Adam and Eve were given the wonderful Garden of Eden to roam in, but were forbidden to eat the apples from one tree. Then they were left free to decide to do so or not. Human reaction to prohibitions being what it is, and egged on by the serpent (see p. 6), they chose to eat the forbidden fruit: Eve first, and she then tempted Adam. (So it was hardly his fault at all really, was it? – this highly sexist story appears to have been devised by males! See the imaginary Byron letter, p. 76: 'It was the woman that bade me eat.') Although the tree in the story is the Tree of the Knowledge of Good and Evil, over the centuries it has become particularly associated with sex. It is a neat late-twentieth-century reversal in this play that the apple is offered to a mature woman by a tongue-tied boy.

According to Newton's physics – the orthodoxy in which Thomasina is being trained (p. 7) – given complete information about the physical state of the universe and all the laws, we could predict the future exactly, and there would be no room for free will. Thomasina adds to this what is really a religious idea: that therefore 'the formula for all the future ... must exist'.

But this leads her (p. 49) to feel the limitations of the geometry she is studying, with its regular shapes. Most shapes in the world are irregular: she wants to find the equations for them too – striking out with her own free will into what would be now called fractal geometry, a mathematics which might be seen as more Gothic than

175

Classical. Stoppard ties in yet another of the play's themes by having her choose the leaf of an apple as an example, thus associating in our minds the geometry of irregular forms with the vagaries of (see below) 'the attraction that Newton left out'.

Chaos

This final state sounds rather like our traditional first state – primeval chaos (Genesis: 'without form, and void'). The word 'chaos' has gradually come to mean wild disorder – as in a Gothic landscape. Its use to identify the modern science of **chaos theory** can be misleading. Chaos theory shows not that there is no order to things, but that certain iterative (repeating) processes in mathematics – while they are simple to define and perfectly deterministic – give rise to constantly changing graphs of results which appear to have no *recognisable* order, and so look as if they are randomly generated. Thomasina is looking at a leaf and dreaming of the iterated algorithm (a process where the output becomes the next input) which might produce it. Valentine is starting with statistics and trying to find the algorithm behind them.

Chaos theory is not in itself Gothic and terrifying; nor does it contradict determinism. What it does show is that things are considerably more complicated than was thought in Newton's day – or even in the mid-twentieth century, when some imagined themselves to be on the verge of finding (see p. 62) 'A theory of everything'. Chaos theory subverts such premature hopes with findings that may always look 'chaotic': 'the future is disorder'. But not everyone finds this bad news. Valentine has already said that it 'makes me so happy', and now adds that this is 'the best possible time to be alive'. Since chaos mathematics – in Stoppard's own later words to Mel Gussow (*Conversations with Stoppard*, December 1994, p. 84) – 'is precisely to do with the unpredictability of determinism', it seems to offer at least temporary relief to those, such as this dramatist, who instinctively resist determinism's tyrannic certainties.

The Portfolio

The stage-note to p. 56 identifies three vital items which have survived in Septimus's portfolio, to be scrutinized 180 years later by Hannah and Valentine: a primer (or textbook), a lesson-book (or exercise book: the writing in it is Thomasina's own), and a diagram, also by her, hurriedly sketched on pp. 113–15.

The **primer** contains Thomasina's marginal claim to have found 'the New Geometry of Irregular Forms'. Near the end of the play, three years later, she says this was only a thirteen-year-old's joke, parodying what she believed to have been the similar 'joke' of Fermat.

Yet later generations have not found Fermat to be joking; and for much of the play we are tempted to believe Thomasina's claim, since Valentine is impressed by her **lesson-book**. But what impresses him is work she was doing three years later, at sixteen: there, her iterated algorithms are indeed on the right road towards modern fractal geometry. She couldn't go far down that road; but when Valentine puts her equations through his computer they appear 'beautiful': 'the Coverly set' (a sly comparison with the real-life 'Mandelbrot set'). Thomasina was a genius without the equipment she needed.

The **diagram** is on a quite different topic. On the last

evening of Thomasina's life Septimus shows her (p. 108) an essay from Paris about heat-flow. She is instantly absorbed by it, and on pp. 113–15 rushes off a diagram which shows that Noakes's engine 'repays eleven pence in the shilling at most'. Septimus complains (p. 116) that this isn't stated anywhere in the French essay, and Thomasina agrees: she 'noticed it by the way'. As may indeed happen to a scientist of genius, someone else's work has triggered a further perception of her own: at thirteen she was already puzzled that she couldn't *un*stir the jam in her rice pudding.

Rice Pudding and the Steam Pump

That seemed to her 'odd', then, because, in Newtonian physics, any process that can flow one way in time can also flow the other. Septimus (p. 6) hasn't transferred his Newton to everyday life and so doesn't find it odd at all. The same pattern of words is repeated, on a similar subject, by Valentine and Hannah on p. 104:

VALENTINE: ... Your tea gets cold by itself, it doesn't get hot by itself. Do you think that's odd?
HANNAH: No.
VALENTINE: Well, it is odd.

It takes a sharp and original mind to notice the oddity of what is familiar. On p. 116, Septimus, though a graduate in science from Cambridge, sees nothing interesting in the fact that 'Mr Noakes's engine cannot give the power to drive Mr Noakes's engine'; he merely says that 'Everybody knows that.' 'Yes, Septimus,' says Thomasina, who is now more or less tutoring *him*, 'they know it about engines!' Her mind has leapt ahead to the implications of the French discovery that 'the atoms do not go according to Newton', in an intuition of the second law of thermodynamics, expounded by Valentine (p. 104): 'we're all going to end up at room temperature'. All energy will be degraded to the same level: everything is gradually running down. Finally, nothing will be distinguishable from anything else or able to act upon it; nothing will *happen* any more.

What Drives Septimus Mad?

'Proofs that the world was coming to an end'; these, according to Hannah on p. 36, were 'stacked solid' in the hermitage after Septimus's death. And the fictional letter from Thomas Love Peacock to Thackeray (p. 87) says that 'Frenchified mathematick brought him to the melancholy certitude of a world without light or life'; but that 'the proof of his prediction [was] even yet unyielding to his labours.' In other words, Septimus was following up Thomasina's diagram, trying to prove what would later be discovered as the second law of thermodynamics.

Yet Peacock adds that these labours were 'for the restitution of hope through good English algebra'. This suddenly suggests that perhaps Septimus was rather trying to *disprove* 'the melancholy certitude'. And on p. 104, echoing the phrase 'good English algebra' on p. 87, Valentine also says that Septimus was trying 'to save the world', rather than prove it 'doomed'. As he speaks he is looking not at the diagram (about heat exchange) but at the lesson-book: Thomasina's iterated algorithm which she calls (p. 103) her 'rabbit equation' because 'it eats its own progeny'. This is the 'Coverly set' which, when pushed through Valentine's computer, produces (p. 101) 'in an ocean of ashes, islands of order. Patterns making themselves out of nothing.' Studying the equation, Septimus believes 'It will go to infinity or zero'. Then he adds 'or nonsense', but this Thomasina denies: 'No, if you set apart the minus roots they square back to sense.' (Don't worry: even to a mathematician this line borders on science fiction, since we can't see her equation.)

A few minutes later, she finds Septimus brooding not on the equation but on the page in his (and her) old primer where she mischievously wrote, in imitation of Fermat, her claim to have 'found a truly wonderful method'. She has perhaps forgotten even making this 'joke', but Septimus senses a link (which Valentine can confirm: today, if you want to 'draw' a leaf on a computer screen, you use iterated algorithms). And even before her death he is becoming hooked: 'It will make me mad as you promised.'

Thermodynamics (the diagram) and chaos theory (the lesson-book, and indeed the 'joke' in the primer) are quite separate fields; but Thomasina left clues to both, and Septimus may have gone mad trying not merely to follow them up but to *reconcile* them. Conceivably the 'patterns making themselves out of nothing' might show how the running-down of the world could reverse itself. (I am told that similar speculations are still sometimes made.) Valentine – the voice we should presumably trust – insists there is no hope of this: 'there's an order things can't happen in'. *Our* world is definitely 'doomed. But if this is how it started, perhaps it's how the next one will come.'

As elsewhere in Stoppard, these are ideas that cannot be done justice within the play; those interested need to pursue them beyond. But at least in the theatre everyone grasps that Thomasina had the notions of a genius but not the equipment to try them out; and neither did the agonised Septimus. And it is Septimus who tells her (p. 50) that we should not grieve

> for your lesson book which will be lost when you are old ... What we let fall will be picked up by those behind. The procession is very long and life is very short. We die on the march. But there is nothing outside the march so nothing can be lost to it ... Mathematical discoveries glimpsed and lost to view will have their time again.

Of course there is another and more obvious reason why Septimus goes mad trying to develop Thomasina's intuitions: his bitter ironic remorse for having acted so honourably on that final night. If he had accepted her invitation to go to her room she might never have died.

'The Attraction that Newton Left Out'

Lady Croom on p. 95 remarks to Septimus that 'It is a defect of God's humour that he directs our hearts everywhere but to those who have a right to them.' Chloe on p. 97 makes much the same suggestion, summed up by Valentine as 'The attraction that Newton left out. All the way back to the apple in the garden.'

This is another kind of 'chaos': a magnetism that helps to invigorate Stoppard's plot and draw its more intellectual material together. The underlying scheme is as elaborate as in a farce: almost every character is partly driven or perplexed by sexual feeling. Furthermore, such couplings as do occur aren't satisfyingly mutual. Septimus has sex with Mrs Chater but feels little or nothing for her, Lady Croom's admission of him to her bedroom may be mainly to console herself for the loss of Byron, and Bernard has scant feeling for Chloe, while Mrs Chater and Byron are surely simply addicted to the sport itself rather than to any particular matters.

It may be useful to revise these complications, in the characters' order of appearance:

Thomasina at thirteen is curious about sex, and at sixteen dreams of marrying Byron, but discovers in the play's intensely erotic and poignant final minutes that she is actually in love with Septimus, who 'cannot . . . will not' reciprocate.

Septimus is initially in trouble over Mrs Chater, but not remotely in love with her. His secret passion is for his employer, Lady Croom – feelings he assumes can never be requited or even declared: he confines them to a letter to be read only after his death. Lady Croom disobeys this instruction and reads it anyway; after briefly pretending to be offended, she is soon inviting Septimus to her room. Three years later, her interest in Count Zelinsky makes Septimus 'sulk'.

Mr Noakes may be a voyeur, his spy-glass trained on the gazebo not by chance.

Lady Croom probably sleeps with Byron and soon afterwards allows Septimus to come to her. In 1812 she appears in public in London simultaneously with him and Count Zelinsky; and back in Derbyshire, even while dallying with the Count, keeps Septimus also on a string (p. 111, 'do not despair of it').

Captain Brice is obsessed with Mrs Chater, which (see p. 95) is why Chater gets to discover his dahlia, and then to die.

Chloe falls heavily for Bernard, who is twice her age; he casually sleeps with her but as quickly drops her. The person he invites to London 'for sex' is Hannah, with whom Valentine is (hopelessly) in love, as also is his fifteen-year-old brother Gus – whose ancestor Augustus at the same age feels the need to ask Septimus about 'carnal matters' (thus setting up a minor symmetry).

The offstage characters include not only the promiscuous Mrs Chater and Byron, but also the *present-day* Lady Croom, who in a pleasant additional flick is described as being 'in a flutter about Bernard' and has lent him her bicycle ('a form of safe sex').

It is an ingeniously wrought series of frustrations, without ever becoming farcical: each appears realistic enough as we hear of it. The person who seems to escape is Hannah. She believes she has put sex firmly in its place: 'nothing against it' but 'it gets less important'. Having declined various offers of marriage she remains free 'to fart in bed' – a deliberate crudity to display how contemporary and up-front she is about the whole thing. But Valentine tells Bernard that 'she won't let anyone kiss her', and tells Hannah herself, with a lover's insight, that 'Your classical reserve is only a mannerism; and neurotic.' He senses that sexual attraction may be as problematic for Hannah, in her refusal to accept it, as for its more obvious victims.

She might say, as such people often do, that all her 'love' is channelled into her work, on the Sidley Park hermit. But there she seems destined to be as frustrated as anyone, until the final moments of the play when she is handed the proof she needs, Thomasina's final drawing of 'Septimus with Plautus'. It comes as a present from Gus, the awkward silent adorer whose knowledge of the house and family effectively bridges the centuries, just as on stage he is visually indistinguishable from his ancestor.

He may have understood that Hannah cannot accept his love; but now, as if guided by some paranormal knowledge, he is able to give her what she wants most, what she really was 'looking for'.

Characters

Within Stoppard's work overall, and despite the intricacies of its long final scene, *Arcadia* is a relatively realist play. There are affectionate echoes of earlier English comedy; but this is not Stoppard in travesty mode. In general both past and present are intended to be plausible, and the perceptions and idiom of the characters are true to their period: even when Thomasina is rebellious in wanting to 'plot' a leaf (p. 49), she is working on rationalist assumptions, true to her upbringing, that its 'equation' must exist and can be found.

Captain Brice and Mr Noakes are as convincing as they need to be in their brief appearances on stage. Ezra Chater is more of an exaggeration, along the lines of characters in Ben Jonson's plays nearly four hundred years earlier – blinded by praise of his poetry to the same speaker's admission of misconduct with his wife. Maybe the truth is that Chater knows his wife's chastity is a lost cause but still entertains hopes for his writing.

If one character seems drawn more from literature than from life it is Lady Croom. We are told she is in only her mid-thirties, and for Septimus to be so smitten with her she must have physical charms which don't appear in her speech: her tongue has the sharp fluency of a possibly much older woman, blistering, for example, to Septimus on p. 92, at other times providing dismissals not a million miles from those of Lady Bracknell – e.g., on p. 15, 'Do not dabble in paradox, Edward, it puts you in danger of fortuitous wit.' (That the numbskull Captain Brice is her brother takes a bit of believing.) Theatrically, her function is to dominate the scenes in which she appears, and to provide verbal pirouettes like those of the best Restoration or eighteenth-century comedy:

> His head is full of Lisbon and Lesbos, and his portmanteau of pistols ... The whole of Europe is in a Napoleonic fit, all the best ruins will be closed. (p. 54)

But that Septimus is in love with her – and remains so for more than three years, in his early twenties – is a *donnée*, a fictional fact we have to accept without having it fully created for us.

Another such *donnée* is Thomasina's genius. But in every other respect she appears at the start of the play as an entirely convincing thirteen-year-old, curious not only about sex but about what's for dinner, and darting (p. 18) from thoughts of death to adding a hermit to the sketch of the hermitage and instantly then on to Septimus's feelings for her mother. When she reappears on the eve of her seventeenth birthday, she has become a dangerous pupil, building an intrigue ('I told him you kissed me. But he will not tell', p. 107) out of a child's-play 'compact' which she probably suggested herself. For more than three years Septimus has been her sparring partner in mental activity – the most exciting part of her life; he is young and virile and has recently returned from 'waltzing like mice' in London. It was also he who first informed her about sex and whom she promised, 'when I am grown to practise it myself I shall never do so without thinking of you.' She can fantasise about marrying Byron, but the person she is setting up, without fully realising what she is doing, is her tutor. The fact that she is now so far ahead of him mathematically may also confirm her feelings of maturity: it is a woman rather than a girl, perhaps, who says on the penultimate page, 'I will wait for you to come.'

Septimus himself is no angel. He is the nearest we come to seeing his friend Byron on stage; they are of the same age, both are attractive to women, and they display similar acuteness, social poise, bravado and (notably to Chater on p. 9) sexual arrogance. That said, we should note the differences between them. Septimus is a bit of a dandy, but more of a Stoppardian would-be-good. Admittedly he feels no scruples about his assignations with Mrs Chater, whom he has done nothing to corrupt; and he enters into an affair with his employer, Lady Croom – but only after, against his intentions, she discovers his suppressed feelings for her: it is, on his side, a genuine love affair. Whatever our view of this, we may sense instinctive moral decency in the lightness, and also firmness, with which Septimus handles adolescent curiosity about sex, in Thomasina and later in her young brother. And this makes believable his reaction to the severe moral test which faces him in the closing pages of the play, as Thomasina offers herself to him. He is surely tempted (p. 127: '*He kisses her again, in earnest.*'). But in his last words, on p. 129, he insists not only on his professional ethics as her tutor – 'I cannot ... I may not' – but also finally (with intense relevance to one of the issues of the whole play) on his own personal moral free will: 'I will not.'

Moral seriousness is much more, of course, than sexual propriety. Where Septimus seems also unlike Byron is in his concern, strengthened by Thomasina, for knowledge: the quite unironic pursuit of scientific and mathematical truth. Like Hannah (p. 100) he might say: 'It's wanting to know that makes us matter.' And again there is a fierce poignancy in the plot: Byronic cynicism would have saved Septimus from going mad. Valentine is exhilarated by the passing of outmoded perceptions of order: 'the future is disorder ... It's the best possible time to be alive' (p. 63). And the play itself, in its intricacy and its humour, tends to endorse this exhilaration. But it carries within it one grim casualty: Septimus, the youthful, elegant and gifted product of the Enlightenment, is transformed to a lunatic hermit, 'twenty years without discourse or companion' (p. 87), and dies aged forty-seven, 'hoary as Job and meagre as a cabbage-stalk', a figure of Gothic gloom and extremity.

Of the present-day characters, two are easily grasped and understood. Chloe believes herself to be thoroughly sophisticated – about sex, which she sees as more or less everything; but when Bernard starts his getaway (p. 127) her response is that of traditional high romance: 'I'll come with you' (as it were lovers fleeing away into the storm); and his brusque, 'No, you bloody won't' reduces her to instant tears, suddenly a vulnerable eighteen-year-old. Bernard propels much of the stage-action with his selfish energy, which makes him theatrically attractive, but only in the tradition of Mr Toad: audiences have always enjoyed seeing such swaggerers stumble, blinkered by their own self-interest. At the start of the long final scene Bernard is being celebrated in the national press, but he is reduced later to a buffoon's absurdity, pulling 'something like a bishop's mitre ... completely over his face' rather than be photographed by even a local newspaper. His chosen subject is Byron and he might dream of himself as a Romantic: on p. 66 he explicitly rejects both reason and science, but does so crudely and unconvincingly, and his refusal to heed Hannah's (rational) cautions leads to his deserved come-uppance. Ironically (blind Cupid again) he finds her attractive even while he tries to mock or contest everything she believes in. To her, meanwhile, even his deviousness is transparent, for example when 'He becomes instantly po-faced' (p. 65).

Valentine is the play's Stoppardian innocent, the descendant of Mr Moon – but also, in his mathematical understanding, its most informed voice. The Coverlys today tend to be living off their past (a fair observation about some aristocratic families): the modern Lady Croom retraces the former gardens, her batty husband resists Japanese cars and anything typewritten, and the tongue-tied Gus spends hours in the library, 'going through' the old 'stuff'. And although Valentine is 'technically' a post-graduate student at Oxford, he spends his time at home and has chosen to work on the old game books of his own family. In terms of maths and information technology he is the most up-to-date of the characters, but he seems to be avoiding the outside world (and that, too, is a fair observation about some computer freaks).

But the real reason he spends so much time at home may be the presence there of Hannah: it is plain that he is another victim of (p. 95) the 'defect in God's humour'. The 'joke' that Hannah is his fiancée is as potentially painful as the 'jokes in the margin' that Thomasina reckons she finds in Fermat and creates herself. And in psychological terms Hannah is the play's central enigma – central because it is her work that gradually unearths the main plot, the tragic story of Thomasina and Septimus; and paradoxically central because, though two of the three present-day males are in love with her and the third,

Bernard, at least wants sex with her, she is determined to remain uninvolved. They spin agitated round her flame while she (see discussion in this book, p. 183) 'won't let anyone kiss her', and later is excluded – presumably at her own wish, but this isn't made clear – from the group photograph, p. 121.

Finally, though, and in some ways most crucially, Hannah is central because she sums up for us the tension in 1809 between the Classical and the Gothic-Romantic. The big speech is on p. 36–7: in Hannah's view things started to go wrong with Sidley Park not just with 'the whole Romantic sham' (say, 1790–1820) but even forty years earlier, in the pretend-natural landscaping of Capability Brown. Her own preference is for 'the whole sublime geometry' of the earlier, highly ornamental gardens; the 1730 engraving shows 'Paradise in the age of reason'. But gradually, she feels, the century 'turned in on itself', in the 'decline from thinking to feeling', the feeling itself not ultimately real but 'cheap thrills and false emotion'. This is the standard anti-Romantic line.

'Paradise', however, suggests the Garden of Eden; and a few pages later Hannah will be offered, by her tongue-tied adorer, an apple. 'Oh dear', is how she ends the scene: any human version of Paradise has to deal with feelings (as any Arcadia must accommodate death), but Hannah would rather not. 'I've always been given credit,' she says wryly on p. 64, 'for my unconcern.' As Bernard's excitement rises, she feels the need to cry, 'Don't kiss me!' and a moment later, p. 65, attempts to deflate him with sarcasm: 'Such passion. First Valentine, now you. It's moving' – clearly the words of someone who prefers not to be 'moved'. She declares that her book on the hermit will be about 'the nervous breakdown of the Romantic

Imagination'; but on p. 99 Valentine will describe her own 'classical reserve' as 'neurotic'. Stoppard, himself a writer accused (though wrongly, in my view) of being short on feeling, is careful to represent not only the 'A' of Hannah's anti-Romanticism but also the 'minus A' of possible psychological diagnosis. What Valentine has learned from chaos theory (pp. 62–3) is that nature is a mixture of classical symmetry (the snowflake) and Romantic blur (the snowstorm); and without preaching a pat 'message' the play quietly suggests that human beings will always need to accept in themselves the same duality: the rational and the emotional.

Stagecraft

Gus and Augustus

These characters, not yet discussed, are persons in their own right but also form a single theatrical device. Teasingly, with a faint shiver of the paranormal, they link the two periods of the play, and prepare for the simultaneity of the great final scene.

They are, of course, boys of the same age, the one a direct descendant of the other and identical to look at, being played by the same actor. One of them, Augustus, is a thoroughly normal fifteen-year-old of his social class; but this normality is met *second*, and only late on in the play. This is highly characteristic of Stoppard, who – where most writers' plots gradually escalate into extremity – frequently brings us back from the bizarre to the explicable, as if in the end life is better trusted than not. Similarly, Gus – suddenly struck dumb at the age of five (we never learn why) yet gifted with remarkable insight –

exists not in the past, where we might find such 'witchcraft' easier to credit, but in a very down-to-earth modernity where his elder brother's first speeches merely repeat a single swear-word.

The story could have managed passably without either character: Bernard, or Hannah herself, *might* have happened upon the drawing of Septimus and Plautus. What Gus and Augustus bring to the play is partly an increased erotic poignancy – adolescent boys to balance Thomasina; Gus as hopeless lover, Augustus embarrassed about 'carnal matters' – but mainly a heightening of mystery and tension. This works largely through Gus, and in two ways.

A tongue-tied character is more disconcerting on stage – where we always expect to *hear* as well as see – than in film. Perversely, perhaps, this may become the person to whose mind we most long for access. But Gus is interesting even before we know he is dumb, because he is also shy: a character who appears only for speechless seconds soon becomes one we want to see again. Then, on p. 45, his first real action is breathtaking: the offering of the apple.

In myth, disability is sometimes linked to compensatory gifts – senility to wisdom, blindness to paranormal insight or foresight. Gus is a skilful improviser on the piano, an activity which Valentine explicitly compares to searching for a lost algorithm and to Thomasina's 'playing with the numbers'. Often, too, adolescents are credited with psychic sensitivity. 'Magic' of this kind is suggested by Gus's knowledge of the history of Sidley Park, most strikingly when he corrects his mother in her search for Capability Brown's boat-house. Yet of course there is a realistic explanation: an intelligent boy, made shy by his disability, has spent years delving into the house's books and papers. The fact that he can point his mother to the right place seems mysterious only because he is dumb: a speaking fifteen-year-old would simply explain. 'It's in the old plans in the library, isn't it?'

Nothing in *Arcadia* would interest a psychical researcher, and in fact the play would be weakened if it relied on some imaginary paranormal occurrence. But that doesn't prevent our skin from tightening somewhat in the theatre, which is a place to savour illusion and strange effects; perhaps some part of us, particularly in this place, really wants to believe in the magic. When, quite late in the play, Augustus suddenly appears, physically active and vocally arrogant, we may momentarily wonder whether we are seeing an earlier, unhandicapped Gus, and then whether the modern Gus is perhaps a broody haunting spirit whose real identity is locked in the past. That would be a good yarn, an engaging supernatural tale; even when we know the *rational* explanations, we may savour the *feeling* of insecurity.

Stoppard exploits to the full this theatrical shiver. Firstly, he allows Gus eventually to dress in Regency costume, which he is fervently keen to do, plucking his brother's sleeve on p. 68 (before the play's first act has ended) almost as if his heart lay there in the dressing-up box. Secondly, in an effect carefully delayed till the penultimate page, Gus will be mistaken for his ancestor, apparently overhearing the final exchange between Septimus and Thomasina. Even when we realise this is not the case – that no one actually overheard them – Gus's presence alongside them onstage carries a further suggestion of the paranormal, as if perhaps Gus really does know everything about this house and its history; perhaps his gift of the drawing to Hannah is thus a gentle concession to her, a fragment released from the past.

The single set

There is so much else to admire in *Arcadia* – plotting, wit, characterisation, the folding together of science and art and garden design – that we may underestimate the strength of its stagecraft. The basic principle is simple, yet a considerable challenge: to alternate the time of Augustus with that of Gus, and finally bring both periods together onstage. As often happens in art, solving the technical problem produces the distinctive strength. A film or novel based on this story would be free to ramble anywhere: up and down Sidley Park, or off to both Byron's and Bernard's London. A thin version of such freedom could have been offered onstage, as in Stoppard's 1997 play, *The Invention of Love*, which ranges notionally over fifty-odd years, from the banks of the Styx to Oxford and London and Worcestershire, without attempting realist settings. Much of the tight hold that *Arcadia* takes on us results from the opposite decision: to do it the hard way, by confining all the action to a single, unchanging, realistic room.

The long stage direction on p. 19 expounds the principle. In 1809–12 the room is a bare schoolroom, without creature comforts; and in the present it is similarly bare because (Chloe, p. 21) 'everything's been cleared out': the room will function as a passageway during tonight's dance. Ingeniously, Stoppard turns the problem of minor anachronistic bits and pieces into a theatrical feature: '*By the end of the play the table has collected an inventory of objects*', just as the audience has collected knowledge from both periods. On the other hand, the books and papers are literally unchanged; and the apple and tortoise and pistol shots are neatly doubled, realistic in either time and yet in a way mocking such theatrical realism, Stoppard being a dramatist who has always gone beyond it.

Alternating scenes

Alternating two separate groups of characters in different settings was a standard means in Shakespeare's day both of broadening a play's range and of building up anticipation. In *Arcadia*, of course, one group of characters is actually *investigating* the other. A routine film-device here would be flashback, beginning in the present then modulating to the past; it is typical of Stoppard to do it the other way round, the modern characters arriving unexpectedly.

Each scene discloses additional knowledge, but this increases, instead of dissipating, the tension of future scenes. Thus Byron is simply 'your friend' in Scene One, his identity revealed only in Scene Two; we learn much about the hermit before realising who he was, and then have to wait a good deal longer before learning what drove him mad. As in all the best stories, the more that is revealed the more tension results. By the end of Scene Six (p. 96) it seems that the Byron subplot has been a dead end: he has gone riding off into the dawn. Septimus's story, on the other hand, is still thickening: he now has an assignation with his employer's wife. There must be more to come concerning him and Thomasina, and also concerning mathematics; we also suspect by this time (though the idea still baffles us) that Septimus – he so young and sharp and civilised – is to become the hermit, and that the hermit was obsessed with figures (though why they should be 'Frenchified' is still a mystery). But nobody in the theatre, surely, has guessed exactly what is to come. Every scene so far has been compelling, and up to a point enlightening; yet a considerable amount has been skilfully kept back – including the play's best theatrical effects – for the final scene.

Simultaneity: the final scene

Scene Seven of *Arcadia* seems to me the best thing Stoppard has done. *Rosencrantz* may be his finest *notion* – what the composer Elgar described as the tune that comes just once in a lifetime – but here the theatrical nerve which has always characterised his work is combined with a gripping story. This is a dramatist who generally finds plots hard to develop; but 'With *Arcadia* I got lucky' (to Mel Gussow again, *Conversations with Stoppard*, p. 106). 'The more I got into it, the more I realised that this was going to work as a piece of story-telling.' But talk of 'luck' here understates the eventual achievement. Not only is the story original, but the stagecraft is exceptionally intricate and moving.

The scene starts (p. 96) with an instant mismatch or overlap. The faces we see are those of the present – as we more or less expect, since the periods have generally alternated so far – yet two of these modern characters are dressed in Regency clothes; and so is the third, Gus, or is he? – no, he's trying such costumes on. We are being teased. A few moments later Hannah's 'you all look so romantic' only sharpens the teasing, carrying as it does several complex vibrations. And yet, in spite of the costumes, there is plenty of interest in the 'present-day' action – Valentine still trying to crack Hannah's emotional defences, followed by his new interest in

Thomasina's equations, which he earlier dismissed as 'doodling'. Once again, as when he first discussed her figures, piano improvisation is heard. 'Patterns making themselves out of nothing.'

Hannah then reveals that Thomasina died young. 'Burned to death ... The night before her seventeenth birthday.' We gulp. We pause.

Almost instantly, there Thomasina is onstage, and no one could seem more alive: a furious adolescent chasing her tiresome brother, who looks bewilderingly like Gus. And yet Valentine and Hannah remain alongside. This is breaking the clear previous division of periods on stage: suddenly we are being asked to accept simultaneity. There is no time to brood on this, because in another typically Stoppardian reversal of cliché, the past is not some misty fade-in but a noisy intrusion. These loud children are quite unlike ghosts, and Augustus is neither tongue-tied (he is shouting) nor at all mysterious as he leers at the drawing-class: 'we only draw naked women'. Septimus puts him down shrewdly ('You may work from memory') and requests silence; but soon Thomasina is challenging him with her 'rabbit equation'. Then, as he begins to look again at her work, a modern hand – Hannah's – is turning the pages with him.

This raises the hairs on our spine; the more so because in most ghost stories it is the ghost who intervenes on the present-day character, not this other way around. Meanwhile, what are the words being spoken? – they are about nothing less than the world's 'doom'.

Stoppard's earlier plays, on his own admission, tended to work by a series of 'moments'. Here the moments remain individually gripping and yet the onward movement is always maintained. Gradually we become aware –

unless we have already guessed from Thomasina's manner
– that we are now watching 1812, not 1809. Septimus is
still in residence but Lady Croom has a new toy-boy, a
Polish pianist: it is he rather than Gus now playing
offstage, but the sound is forced to compete with that of a
steam pump and the gardens have become muddy
earthworks. Earlier the apple and tortoise doubled in
different scenes, now Lady Croom's complaint about
'disturbance' equally fits the steam pump and a shout
from the modern Chloe, seeking Gus. (He is probably in
the library, finding for Hannah the portrait of Septimus
and Plautus which we will watch Thomasina draw on
p. 116 and which Augustus – in his real respect for
Septimus – will ask to keep.) Valentine and Chloe leave
but Hannah remains quietly reading; and on p. 111 what
she finds in the garden book (eventually read aloud to us
on p. 119) is the same information the audience hears
from Lady Croom: the two Chaters were one. Bernard has
indeed made a public fool of himself.

The scene is in fact virtually two, the transition
occurring on p. 122. The first, for all the fascination of
Thomasina's equations and the grim revelation of her
death, has been generally boisterous, from 'Bonking
Byron Shot Poet' through the children's chase, the steam
pump, Lady Croom's exasperation and Bernard's dis-
comfiture. But now the stage-set begins to look for the
first time beautiful, as the lights dim and the paper
lanterns outside glow. Stoppard seems to have put all
irony aside, settling for traditional showbiz effects – even
for the fragile sound of a piano heard on an empty stage,
which is something of a cliché. This, a cynic might say, is
what costume drama is *supposed* to be like. Will it last?
In all his previous work, Stoppard would finally have

subverted such an elegiac mood: a dry 'minus A' would be brought rattling in.

Here, that doesn't happen. Here the *story* must dominate and be respected; and will be tough enough to resist the charge of sentimentality. And the effects are appropriate: the lights dim as Septimus is about to study Thomasina's diagram of how everything is running down; and the lanterns outside increasingly suggest stars, a hint of the universe beyond; later there will be fireworks, described significantly in the stage direction as 'like exploding meteors'. The piano is not a cheap stage-effect but has been symbolic throughout, a representation in sound of randomness, and of patterns creating themselves. Later, to mark the re-entry of the present, the piano is replaced by a thumping contemporary beat from the marquee outside, and Valentine lurches in half drunk: nothing sentimental here.

Valentine has just understood Thomasina's diagram. The simultaneity is wound up tighter than ever, as the two scientists together study the diagram, Hannah drinks Septimus's wine (will she too be an unattached hermit-like researcher all her days?) and Thomasina listens to the modern band: 'Is it a waltz now?' allows the audience a laugh, rare in these pages.

We see three different reactions to the running down of the universe. Septimus, a Newtonian all his life, is genuinely shocked, but preserves his usual urbane poise: 'Dear me'. Valentine is learning nothing new, but is fascinated by Thomasina's foresight and enjoys teaching Hannah. And Thomasina – whose presence onstage is always now painful to us, hours away from her death – is fervently excited, thoroughly cheerful about the world's doom but extremely impatient to get waltzing. All three reactions are, we might say, valid: together they make a realistic human composite.

The characters of 1812 waltz to the band of the present day. But we are some way from an ending, and certainly sentimentality continues to be held off, as we witness Bernard's farcical hasty costume-change and his entirely late-twentieth-century brutality to Chloe ('Of course not. What for?'). Then all the modern characters leave except Hannah, whose heart lies in the past and who is still without her proof.

What follows is breathtaking. The waltz ends, in a twirl and a bow. In silent, delicate stage-business Septimus lights Thomasina's candle; by this she will die, in a disastrous transfer of heat. Hannah sits at the table and pours wine, perhaps toying also with some of the objects accumulated there in the course of the overlapping scenes (the stage direction points this up for the reader, but director and actor must find other ways).

The younger people stand looking at each other, on a sexual brink. But he is quietly directing her to bed. 'Be careful with the flame,' Septimus says, though Thomasina must have been handling candles for much of her life. It seems a psychic foreboding on his part, but perhaps he really wants to caution her against the flame of her feelings tonight. As if in answer, she says she will wait for him. In the theatre we may just have time to grasp that if he goes to her, she will not fall asleep waiting for him, with the candle still burning; if he joins her, she need not die. The wrong *moral* decision may by *chance* save a life.

But morally, as her tutor: 'I cannot.'

Thomasina now offers him a permission: 'You may.' But Septimus does not have the permission of his own conscience: 'I may not.' Finally, in what has been ironically a little like a tutorial on auxiliary verbs, the pupil's 'you must' sounds like an assertion of determinism, whereas the tutor's last refusal is an assertion of free will: 'I will not.' With free will goes the obligation of moral choice.

This exchange is electrifying enough, without our additional unease (intended, as the stage-note makes clear) that Lord Augustus may be watching. It is some relief to find that 'he' is modern Gus, and *not* a witness: his eyes are on Hannah. Yet he bridges the centuries in his knowledge of the library: the drawing he hands her shows that Septimus was not only born in the same year as the hermit but also owned the same tortoise. Gus could not have given her a better love-gift, and past events are now fully unravelled.

Thomasina has settled for a further dance with Septimus, and nothing more. Morally we should approve, but it means that death is about to claim her, *even in Arcadia*. Traditional dance allowed impossible couples their possible meetings, in a gracious and tender mode. And here, as two pairs dance together, the past fluent, the present awkward, the play itself is allowed to end in similar grace and tenderness – though also in extreme poignancy.

Arcadia: A Chronology

(fictional events and characters in bold type)

1638–9 Nicolas Poussin's 'Et in Arcadia ego' (a.k.a. 'The Arcadian Shepherds').

mid-1600s Painters Salvator Rosa and Claude Lorraine active; fashion for ornamental geometrical gardens.

1712 Thomas Newcomen's original steam engine.

1727 Death of Isaac Newton.

1740s Horace Walpole's Gothic garden.

mid-1700s Fashion for Capability Brown's landscape designs.

1764 Walpole's *The Castle of Otranto*.

1773 Dr Samuel Johnson travels to the Hebrides.

1787 Birth of Septimus Hodge.

1788 Birth of Byron.

1789–94 French Revolution.

1794 Mrs Radcliffe: *The Mysteries of Udolpho*.

1796 Birth of Lady Thomasina Coverly.

1797 Birth of Lord Augustus Coverly, later Lord Croom.

early 1800s Fashion for 'picturesque' gardens such as those of Sir Humphry Repton (planned in 'garden books').

1809, April Byron at Newstead. *Arcadia*, Scenes 1, 3 and 6. Captain Brice and the Chaters sail for the West Indies.

July Byron sails for European continent.

1810 Ezra Chater discovers dwarf dahlia in Martinique and subsequently dies there of a monkey bite. Captain Brice promptly marries Mrs Chater and brings the dahlia back to England: it is at Sidley Park by October.

1811 Byron returns to Britain. Huge success of 'Childe Harold'. Byron begins affair with Lady Caroline Lamb.

1812 *Arcadia*, Scene 7. Death of Thomasina.

1834 Death of the Sidley Park hermit, Septimus Hodge.

The present (c. 1993) *Arcadia*, Scenes 2, 4, 5, 7.

Textual Notes

Characters
Sidley Park belongs to the Coverly family, whose male head takes the title of Lord Croom. Neither the past nor the present Lord Croom appears on stage, nor does the present Lady Croom. The cast list can be divided historically thus:

1809–12
Lady Croom
Her brother Captain Brice
Her daughter Thomasina (13–16) and son Augustus (seen when 15)
The tutor Septimus Hodge
The butler, Jellaby
Chater, poet, guest of Captain Brice
Noakes, landscaper, employed by Lord Croom

Today
Valentine Coverly, biologist
His sister Chloe (18)
Their brother Gus (15)
Hannah Jarvis, bestselling author
Bernard Nightingale, academic

Act One
SCENE ONE
   2 a shoulder … grouse – 'shoulder' and 'haunch' are normal butchery terms, but 'embrace' is a pun on 'brace' (pair, of hunted animals), and 'hugged' seems to echo 'jugged' (recipe for cooking hare, traditionally another 'game' creature).

- QED – initials of a classic proof in Latin, 'quod erat demonstrandum' (problem solved).
  Gallic Wars – of Caesar: a Latin history book.
  seed fell on stony ground – from Christ's parable of the sower (Matthew 13: 3), this is a traditional tutor's sarcasm about an unreceptive pupil. But Thomasina muddles it – perhaps mischievously – with the 'sin of Onan' who, in the Old Testament, 'spilled' his own *sexual* seed 'upon the ground'.
- Fermat – Pierre de Fermat was a French mathematician of the seventeenth century. His supposed 'last theorem' is summarised by Septimus on p. 4, and his marginal claim for it on p. 7. It was often held to be unprovable, a mistake or even a hoax, until it was eventually proved a few months after *Arcadia* was first performed.
3 gazebo – small garden house in the shape of a lantern.
- landskip – landscape.
- closing the stable door – the proverbial line continues 'after the horse has bolted'.
4 candid – open, honest.
- Ah – Septimus is understandably relieved.
- without thinking of you – Thomasina seems genuinely disgusted, but Septimus sees that if these words came true they might become an extreme compliment; and the audience gets a first faint hint that Thomasina could fall in love with her young tutor.
5 in the gun-room – Chater's letter evidently challenges Septimus to a duel.
6 in the scheme ... as the serpent – in Genesis, the serpent spoils humanity's original bliss in the

Garden of Eden. Snake-like, Noakes spied on and spoiled the bliss of lovers in this garden. Noakes is also an 'improver' of landscape who will spoil the existing 'scheme' of Sidley Park.

- This is known as free will – Septimus is bluffing and changing the subject. The stirring of the jam has in fact nothing to do with free will (on the contrary, 'we *must* stir our way onward', my italics). His tone is almost flippant ('until pink is complete'), as he describes, without any awareness of its significance, evidence of the yet-to-be-discovered second law of thermodynamics (see this book, p. 179). Three years later Thomasina has grasped this significance but Septimus (p. 116) still has not – though after her death he will spend the rest of his life grappling with it.

- Sit! – should get a mild laugh in the theatre, being a command to dogs rather than tortoises. Its real purpose is to draw attention to the fact that Plautus is there at all (he will be important later), and to show instantly certain basic limitations of free will – it only works as long as someone more powerful doesn't shift you around.

- do you think God is a Newtonian? – see discussion above, this book pp. 174–5.

- Etonian – Augustus will later attend England's most prestigious school, Eton.

7 'If everything . . .' – in trying to guess Thomasina's question, Septimus summarises various problems Newtonian physics had presented for theologians. But Thomasina is ahead of him – and everyone else.

9 I demand satisfaction! – i.e., of his honour in a duel. But this offers Septimus an obvious pun.

- epitome – perfect summary.
- Milton – seventeenth-century poet; 'Southey' – contemporary poet (1774–1843).
10 coterie of hacks and placemen – clique of those who write just for money or social position.
- Jeffrey – notoriously fierce critic in the *Edinburgh Review*.
12 a canard – malicious gossip.
- Walter Scott – (1771–1832) the latest bestselling poet (*Marmion* had recently appeared.)
- muddy-mettled – dirty-minded.
- stood up and gave his best on behalf of – Chater is too dim to realise that his words also describe Septimus's 'perpendicular poke' of his wife.
- what do you say, Noakes? – Septimus has turned the disaster intended by Noakes into a triumph. But instantly disaster seems threatened again, by the words of Lady Croom and Brice as they enter.
13 Mr Noakes, this is monstrous! – Septimus assumes Noakes was spying on more than one occasion, while Lady Croom believes Septimus is supporting her objections to Noakes's landscape plans. The misunderstanding continues for most of the page. hyperbolize – exaggerate.
- rape – Brice means this metaphorically – violating the landscape.
- the modern style – Noakes is referring to his designs; Septimus and Chater think he means a decline in sexual morals.
14 Madam ... – Septimus admits making love to Mrs Chater in 'the gazebo' and 'the boat-house', but denies doing so on 'the Chinese bridge' (so conspicuous a place that it must be Noakes's

'fantasy') and is offended to be thought capable of doing so in 'the shrubbery' (too lowly and furtive?).

– thanks to Septimus – the next misunderstanding begins.

– Salvator Rosa – Italian painter, 1615–73. His 'picturesque' style included wild rocky landscapes and ruins.

– How is a ... ruined castle? – Thomasina's mischievous point is that a ruined *building* is fashionably admired.

15 paradox – self-contradicting statement (often intended to show cleverness). On this page Lady Croom emerges as a self-consciously epigrammatic speaker in an eighteenth-century tradition.

– fortuitous – arriving by chance.

– embracing a side of beef – Thomasina realises Septimus may be in trouble for having informed her about sex. To save him, she herself cleverly retreats to the evasive answer he first gave her; and Lady Croom is partly reassured, though 'vulgar curios' (strange objects) is still a rebuke.

– wonderful – the word is carefully chosen: worthy of wonder but not, in this case, approval.

16 rill – stream; 'serpentine' – snaking its way.

– the painter – Nicolas Poussin; see this book, p. 156.

– your geography – Thomasina knows that the real Arcadia (a much rougher landscape than Virgil's idealisation) is in southern Greece.

17 pert – cheeky.

– Mrs Radcliffe – (1764–1823) wrote Gothic novels, the best-known of which is *The Mysteries of Udolpho* (1794). She knew and admired the opinions of Salvator Rosa (see p. 14) and based her horror stories in 'sublime' (i.e., wild and awe-inspiring) landscapes.

- Horace Walpole – (1717–97) made popular both the Gothic novel (*The Castle of Otranto*, 1764) and the Gothic style of landscaping – which is why Noakes is 'thrilled' by his name.

- your friend – in Scene Three we learn this is Byron.

18 the recording angel – in Christian mythology keeps a record of everyone's deeds. This, or simply the 'calendar of slaughter', reminds Septimus of the grimmer meaning of 'Et in Arcadia ego'. Thomasina understands him, and responds with a typical thirteen-year-old's defiance of death ('phooey' is a slang dismissal). But that will prove dramatically ironic: she is to die very young. So will her decision to 'put in a hermit': in fact he is standing there beside her, and, with yet further irony, her thoughts turn instantly and bluntly to him: 'Are you in love with my mother, Septimus?'

- addle the brain? – Thomasina has noticed the contradictions in Mrs Chater's instructions.

19 Baptist in the wilderness – in the New Testament, John the Baptist lived and preached in the wilderness (a Gothic landscape, perhaps) as a forerunner of Christ. Thomasina herself, and Septimus as 'her' hermit, will die as forerunners of late-twentieth-century understanding.

SCENE TWO

20 *theodolite* – instrument used in surveying (here, in rediscovering the lost garden, see pp. 31–2).

21 wrinklies – older generation.

23 commode – any useful piece of furniture

(Valentine's meaning) or (restricted modern usage, and Bernard's) a glorified chamber-pot/portable lavatory.

– Nigh– – Bernard hastily decides to suppress his name now he knows who 'Miss Jarvis' is.

24 No, for reading it – so 'she' here means Valentine's mother, not Hannah.

25 awake – we, of course, expect to hear 'asleep'.

– *Women in Love* – was indeed written by D. H. Lawrence; but the children's *Just William* books certainly weren't, and the *Argus* is just a local newspaper.

– Brighton – home of 'Sussex' University.

– *bonhomie* – social brightness.

26 ha-ha – a ditch, perhaps also with sunken fence, to exclude live-stock without interrupting the view. *The Shorter Oxford Dictionary* favours Bernard's pronunciation, stressing the second syllable.

– old Murray – John Murray (1778–1843), publisher of guide-books.

27 Lady Caroline Lamb – a married woman with whom Byron openly had an affair. The title *Caro* suggests the popular style of Hannah's book about her.

– English don – university lecturer in English literature.

– oeuvre – French for a writer's work; used in English the word sounds pretentious and is therefore here ironic.

28 DNB – *Directory of National Biography*.

– Zilch – nothing.

30 Brideshead Regurgitated – Evelyn Waugh's novel *Brideshead Revisited* deals with the inheritor of a

stately home who also studies at Oxford; Bernard probably regards its characters as enfeebled and out of date. The following few lines – easily overlooked on the printed page – are strong theatre ('Christ' is a gasp of relief.).

– It's a joke – but 'jokes' in this play can be devastating. On p. 8 Thomasina is certain that Fermat's claim was 'a joke to make you all mad'; and later she writes a copy-cat marginal claim of her own, which on p. 123 she assures Septimus was 'a joke' (he replies, accurately, 'It will make me mad as you promised.') Bernard is quick to realise that the 'joke' between Hannah and Valentine may be fairly desperate for Valentine.

– a freebie – at no cost. 'My' is then Bernard pretending to be Valentine.

32 Attagirl – that's the spirit, girl.

33 peg – to hang a book on (common phrase among writers).

– Coleridge – S. T. Coleridge, key poet and theorist of English Romanticism.

– Very biblical – Thomasina (the 'later hand') 'made him look like the Baptist in the wilderness', p. 19. Since she was drawing before there was either hermitage or hermit, this 'only known likeness' is not a likeness at all.

34 Capability Brown – Lancelot 'Capability' Brown (1715–83) designed parks and gardens to look natural (as Hannah will explain on pp. 36–7). 'Claude' Lorraine (1600–82) painted landscapes possibly suggesting the pastoral 'Arcadian' poetry of 'Virgil' (70–19 BC).

– Florence – Bernard instinctively thinks of Florence

Nightingale, celebrated nurse in the Crimean War.

- Thomas Love Peacock – (1785–1866) knew and satirised Romantic writers, and wrote (see p. 35) *Headlong Hall*.
- anchorites – those who withdraw themselves from the world.
- savant – man of learning, particularly in science.
- oxymoron – a phrase which seems to contradict itself (how can a sage be a lunatic?). Bernard is making a terrible pun on 'moron' meaning idiot.

35 Thackeray – W. M. Thackeray (1811–63) was a journalist and novelist, author of *Vanity Fair*.

36 Epiphany – moment of (divine) revelation. Bernard's 'Peg' quotes Hannah back at herself (see p. 33); but this time she comes out with a much flashier word from her 'popular' writing style, and senses no irony in Bernard's 'that's it'.

- cabalistic – coded.

37 Of course – because, in Bernard's view, Hannah thinks in popular cliché.

38 Really? ... interest. Bernard is gradually giving away his real interest. Two of Byron's poems are then mentioned, and 'Newstead' was his family home (see p. 71).

41 the tapes – tying up the book; see p. 1.

42 *raspberry* – puff of scorn.

- as soon as he could find a ship – although duelling was a tradition of honour, any resulting death was still a capital offence (see p. 70): Byron would have to flee the country. (In historical fact, Byron was indeed challenged to a duel over a woman, in Malta later this year, 1809.)

- *this is fame* – i.e., for you and me.

44 a pony – i.e., to keep her mind off sex.

45 it gets less important – Hannah takes Chloe's 'fix you up' to refer specifically to sex.

- Beau Brummel – fashion icon of the Regency period.

- That's a joke! – see p. 30: Hannah assumes Chloe means her *older* brother.

- GUS *has an apple* – in a number of legends an apple is a significant offering, but often also sinister; e.g., Eve's to Adam in the Garden of Eden, the golden apple of discord given by Paris to Aphrodite, the poisoned apple in Snow White … Here the apple's *leaves* will prove directly useful.

SCENE THREE

46 Plautus – (the name of a Roman poet) is in English traditionally pronounced to rhyme with 'tortoise'. The audience does not hear the name till p. 85 (see note on that page).

- SEPTIMUS *reading a letter* – it is clear later that the letter Septimus has just received via Jellaby is Chater's second (the third letter read aloud on p. 41).

- THOMASINA *is studying* – Septimus has given Thomasina a passage from the Roman historian Plutarch, without telling her that it is the basis for one of Shakespeare's finest speeches (*Antony and Cleopatra* II.ii.195). On p. 51 he pretends the Shakespeare is his own translation.

- for the post – i.e., the mail, not for someone at Sidley Park.

49 A gibe is not a rebuttal – a jeering remark does not

prove a theory wrong. Thomasina makes a good guess at why Septimus is 'churlish'; but he also knows he must face Chater again, now doubly offended. Her shrewdness about other people's amorous emotions (including her own mother's on the previous page) seems relatively untroubled, partly because she is (p. 19) *'an uncomplicated girl'* but also because she has other more intellectual questions on her mind, as is very clear in 'let them elope ... knowledge'. She is dissatisfied with the limitations of 'commonplace' geometry, with its rigid man-made look ('shapes of manufacture', 'cabinet'). If those shapes have equations, so must all other shapes, in 'God's truth'.

50 a Ptolemy – i.e., a member of Cleopatra's family.

 – the enemy – the Roman Empire, which (though long after Cleopatra) destroyed the great library and the texts within it. Thomasina lists the three great Greek dramatists and the philosopher Aristotle.

 – But instead ... – Thomasina's speech and Septimus's reply represent dramatic irony at its most agonising. She is a genius with visions of future developments in mathematics, and she is to die in a fire, though her 'lesson book', which Septimus assumes will be lost, will in fact survive. After her death he will be unable to muster the philosophical calm he recommends here.

51 Archimedes – (297–212 BC) Greek scientist who among other things invented the Archimedean screw, a device to raise water; hence the 'corkscrew' joke.

 – on papyrus – i.e., by ancient Greeks.

53 Tush, sir! – a mild rebuke (Chater has finally grasped that Septimus was insulting his writing), but Brice turns it into an obscene pun. He is keener to destroy Septimus than to defend Chater: see bottom of p. 11 and also p. 56.

54 That is my copy, madam – this is as far as Septimus feels he can go in protest – Lady Croom is a powerful woman. There is an immediate risk that Chater will tell her of Septimus's misconduct with his wife, and the book contains three letters which would confirm it – Septimus can hardly ask permission to extract them now in front of Chater. On p. 55 he watches her go; when he turns back his mood has changed.

– Mr Hodge ... – to take Lady Croom's long speech as realist, we would need to assume she has modelled her style on the dramatists Congreve (1670–1729) and Sheridan (1751–1816). But she also anticipates Oscar Wilde, and is allowed one foretaste of the twentieth century: 'all the best ruins will be closed.'

– packet – mail-boat which also took passengers;

– portmanteau – suitcase.

– take command of his pistols – this assists Stoppard's plot (the scholar Septimus probably doesn't possess pistols of his own) and also provides a good stage-moment as Chater reacts.

– His lameness – Byron was in fact lame from birth.

55 Ovid – (43 BC–AD 18) Roman love poet.

– ball – shot from a pistol.

– off to the Malta packet – see note to p. 42: Septimus would have to flee the country; Byron ('penurious' means 'short of money') would stay as tutor, which in view of Thomasina's perceptions on p. 48 might well leave Lady Croom 'satisfied'.

56 *the flaw* – since Brice is the second on Septimus's duelling schedule, he can only 'let the air out of him' if Chater is already dead.

SCENE FOUR

56 *the portfolio ... three items* – the *three items* are discussed above, this book p. 177.

– This margin being too mean – exactly like Fermat (p. 7), Thomasina has written in the margin of a printed book (Septimus's maths text-book – 'primer') claiming a discovery explained elsewhere.

57 *a piano ... improvisationally* – the player, it turns out on p. 63, is the tongue-tied Gus. His ability to improvise is not surprising if he's as clever as Chloe thinks; and musically improvisation suggests both free will and the randomness of chaos theory.

– iterated algorithm – an algorithm (named after Arab mathematician Al-Khwarizmi) is a process with an input and an output. If the output is then fed back into the process, the algorithm is said to be 'iterated': see Valentine, 'eats its own numbers' (p. 60) and Thomasina, 'eats its own progeny' (p. 103).

58 Gus loves going through it. No old masters ... – a rational explanation of why Gus will prove so knowledgeable about Sidley Park: compare pp. 64 and 103. 'Old masters' would be valuable paintings, which might be found amongst jumble.

– Why are you cross? – Hannah rightly senses that Valentine is rattled by Thomasina's brilliance: even jealous of it. See also, p. 61, 'Not a schoolgirl ...'

He doesn't want to believe she may have made a breakthrough.

60 Like a piano in the next room – Gus's improvisation may be unconsciously seeking a 'lost algorithm'; see Valentine on the monkey.

61 A monkey at a typewriter – the traditional notion is that given infinity, jabbing the keys at random, a monkey would eventually produce Shakespeare's plays.

62 the snowflake and the snowstorm – perfect and intricate symmetry (as it were, an eighteenth-century design) and a wild alarming randomness (as it were, Gothic).

– Relativity and quantum – advances in physics in the early twentieth century.

– A theory of everything – was indeed the aim of the twentieth-century physicist Einstein (1879–1955). Valentine proceeds to give a sketch of chaos theory.

63 Everything you have to lose – Valentine's feelings for Hannah are not a 'joke'.

– corn in Egypt – Exodus 42: 1: Valentine knows about climate change.

64 Gus put her right – discussed in this book, pp. 191–2.

– good breeding – it is 'good breeding' not to be nosy about a disability, but Hannah says that what others see in her is 'unconcern'. We are learning that she dislikes shows of emotion.

65 Such passion ... moving – not only will Hannah not let anyone kiss her, but she is sarcastic about all displays of feeling, even on intellectual matters.

– po-faced – deliberately blank in expression.

66 visceral – of the guts. Bernard in this speech

consciously sets himself up against Hannah's 'classical' preference for 'reason' over 'passion'. She has rightly pointed out that he has 'established' nothing; his tactic – itself a gut instinct – is to present this defiantly as some sort of virtue.

time is reversed – rather similarly, Bernard seems also out to pick a fight with the scientist Valentine; even Bernard is likely to know that 'reversed' is just what time can't be – though of course he doesn't know how important the idea will prove to be later in the play.

67 My mother's lent him her bicycle – the present Lady Croom may be naturally generous; but the main point is that, like almost everyone else in the play, she has not escaped 'the attraction that Newton left out'.

– Horace Walpole – because she collects gardening books (see note to p. 17).

– Galileo – Galileo Galilei (1564–1642), Italian scientist and astronomer.

68 Do you mean – Valentine's description of someone in the past covering 'thousands of pages' sounds like Hannah's hermit.

– GUS *is plucking* ... – Gus's impatience to get to the dressing-up box again shows his feeling for the past. you'd have to have a reason – as, of course, Septimus did.

– you'd have to be insane – again suggests the hermit.

69 *From a long way* ... – the act ends with the early morning 'pistol shot', plausibly modern yet sending the audience off to the Interval anticipating the 1809 duel.

Act Two

SCENE FIVE

70 'Did it happen? . . .' – Stoppard's *Travesties*, nearly twenty years earlier, also begins Act Two with an informative lecture. In this case, fact and fiction are blurred together.

71 holograph – handwriting.

– *Hannah!* Shut up! – Chloe's constant defence of Bernard in the next few pages, and her tears on p. 82, are explained on p. 85 – she and Bernard have had sex together.

75 clairvoyant – able to see the future.

76 platonic – non-existent ideal. Byron was indeed in Albania in September of 1809.

– it was the woman who bade me eat – Adam's defence to God after eating the apple Eve gave him: the original male evasion of (sexual) blame.

78 I'm Marie of Romania – a mocking line from the American humorist Dorothy Parker, meaning 'Oh yeah?'

– *fame* – see p. 42. Bernard's only fame will be as fool.

79 pan – review harshly.

80 It's a technical term – i.e., from mathematics. This introduces a clash of ideas such as occurs in many Stoppard plays.

81 Don't feed the animals – i.e., don't provoke me. Bernard's previous speech abbreviated the debate: he'll accept science's positive achievements, 'penicillin and pesticides', if Valentine will accept the negatives of 'the bomb and aerosols'. But Chloe's mind doesn't move that fast.

- the lot of you – i.e., scientists; 'the one in the wheelchair' is presumably the physicist Stephen Hawking.
- 'She walks in beauty ...' – the lines are by Byron.

82 Well, I think ... not among pros – Bernard has managed to upset everyone except the tortoise. He moves among professional arguers not easily reduced to tears: see Hannah to Valentine on p. 86.

83 Henry Fuseli – (1741–1825) Romantic artist, often in a Gothic style. But Stoppard is laying one of his ambushes: p. 113 will show that Hannah is right and the 'Fuseli expert' wrong.

85 She meant well – remembering p. 44, Hannah assumes Chloe asked Bernard to come as Hannah's partner.
- Sub rosa – secretly.
- Seduced her ... gave in – compare p. 44 'If you don't want him, I'll have him.'
- something between her legs – i.e., on the shelves. This is pure Stoppard: the apparently outrageous turns out to be literally true and innocent – though no doubt Bernard enjoys the innuendo.
- Plautus by name – this is the first time the tortoise is named, and we have to wait till p. 117 to be absolutely sure it refers to Septimus's pet.

86 a feature – i.e., of Sidley Park.

87 labours for the restitution of hope – see discussion this book pp. 179–80.
- the second law of thermodynamics – see discussion this book p. 179.

88 Did Bernard ... – he means that Hannah seems to have been 'infected' by Bernard's tendency to leap to historical conclusions.

SCENE SIX

88 A reprise – a theatrical repeat – here, of p. 69. When
    Septimus enters, we think he has won the duel; this
    seems confirmed when he produces pistols. When he
    produces a *'dead rabbit'* ... we have been
    ambushed.

90 a book – the inscribed copy of Chater's poem,
    which Bernard believes to be Byron's.

 – not a coin – traditionally a tip was left in this way
    by departing guests.

91 All this to shoot a hare? – Lady Croom is fully
    aware that the duel was planned but did not take
    place. Mockingly she suggests that the only outcome
    of Byron's stay at Sidley Park (and indeed it will be
    the only historical record) is one shot hare (noted
    on p. 66, but even that will be ironically thrown in
    doubt on p. 106). As it happens, Septimus has used
    the early morning to shoot a rabbit, but she is far
    from amused when he offers that as his stalling
    reply.

92 a rake and a hypocrite – a promiscuous man and a
    false-faced one. Lady Croom is personally stung.

 – the Levant – the eastern Mediterranean, where Lady
    Croom implies that morals are lower.

 – your trollop – Mrs Chater.

 – Who else? – Lady Croom betrays her own
    deviousness, unaware that Septimus has already
    heard a distinctly different account. According to
    the butler, Mrs Chater was actually met
    ('encountered' was Jellaby's diplomatic word) 'on
    the threshold of Lord Byron's room', and not by Mr
    Chater, who was carousing downstairs, but by Lady
    Croom herself. No doubt it was then correct of her

to 'despatch' the Chaters, and perhaps Byron himself; but why exactly did she then 'look for' Septimus in his room?

93 *this threat* – Septimus has said he will get Byron to 'give an account'. That seems likely to include assignations with Lady Croom herself.

94 The philosophers ... idle hour – sarcastic and yet flattering; her last line, says Septimus, shows such cleverness that the Athenian philosophers could have learned from it; while the sculptors would have wanted to sculpt her beauty.

– the Indies – the West Indies (we learned on p. 29 that a botanist called Chater died on Martinique).

– She did not tell you? – the voyage has evidently been planned for some time.

95 The Linnean Society – would classify new-found plants.

– Indeed, madam. (*Pause.*) – because Septimus's heart is 'directed' to her.

– ink ... pen ... noticeboard – Septimus had sex with Mrs Chater shortly before writing his letter of adoration to Lady Croom. Thus far the 'ink' is literal; but next moment Lady Croom's heated imagination finds 'pen' and 'dipped' sexually suggestive, and makes Mrs Chater a locality where men's 'writings' are publicly known.

– unrelieved desire – i.e., for you.

96 spare them an hour – i.e., you (notionally, to tell me about them). This is the man whom on p. 92 she was dismissing ('bags packed ... one before you').

– Bring a book – for appearance's sake.

SCENE SEVEN

96 *Regency* – the period 1811–20.

97 'Even in Arcadia' – the headline agrees with Septimus's translation (p. 18).

– do you think … haven't said yet – compare the same pattern of speeches on pp. 6–7.

– the only thing going wrong – compare 'defect in God's humour', p. 95.

– attraction – Newton dealt in physical forces such as gravitational attraction (in popular tradition, revealed to him by the fall of an apple). But 'sexual' attraction is like the 'apple' sinfully taken and eaten in the 'Garden' of Eden.

98 Don't be ridiculous – Bernard will have sent out press releases. Hannah's next words offer another startling insight into the eccentric Lord Croom; the man who never answers typewritten letters and hates Japanese cars nevertheless reads a tabloid.

– What a fool – though Chloe thinks Hannah is just 'jealous' of his successful publicity, Hannah's later 'It can't prove to be true' shows she is absolutely convinced Bernard is wrong; but is also 'like science' because science can only be verified on particular occasions: no general scientific 'truths' can be proved (whereas in mathematics they can). There is no 'proof' that the sun will rise tomorrow.

– You all look so romantic – Hannah is of course using this adjective in its loose popular sense, and implies praise. But the costumes are those of the Romantic period of which she disapproves, and 'You all' is keeping her distance.

99 Science and religion – Valentine thinks that Hannah will 'disappoint' him by taking the (to him old-

fashioned) line that belief in science is incompatible with religious faith.

- I don't know when – echoes Lady Croom's 'I do not know when ...' on p. 96.

- Your classical reserve – neurotic – this, from the man who loves her, is a thoughtful accusation, and neatly reverses Hannah's attribution of neurosis – 'nervous breakdown' – to the 'Romantic Imagination' (p. 33).

100 ... how beautiful! – Valentine is making iterated algorithms ('beautiful' to look at) from Thomasina's equations, which he calls 'the Coverly set' by analogy with the most celebrated example in this field, also named after its discoverer, the 'Mandelbrot set'.

101 ocean of ashes – this is the hermit's 'world without light or life' (see p. 87) which the second law of thermodynamics ultimately implies. But the idea of patterns 'making themselves out of nothing' faintly hints at a contrary potential; compare p. 103 ('how the next one will come') and the discussion above, this book p. 180.

- *The piano starts to be heard* – presumably Gus is playing, but as the two time-periods blend it will become Count Zelinsky.

102 LORD AUGUSTUS, *fifteen* ... – the Regency clothes worn by Valentine and Chloe for the dance have prepared the overlapping of periods which now takes place. The characters from the past and the characters from today show no awareness of each other; this is both theatrically gripping and a challenge to actors, for example when (next page) Septimus and Hannah turn pages of the same book.

Any juxtaposition of past and present tends to carry with it some poignancy: these lively young people are long dead. But, more specifically, Thomasina's costume and manner indicate to the audience that she has grown, and is now close to her seventeenth birthday, on the eve of which (we now know) she died.

– smirking about something – this is revealed on p. 107: 'I told him you kissed me.'

103 my rabbit equation – if the offspring of a rabbit seems too weak to live, the rabbit may eat it (thus conserving energy). Thomasina describes her iterated equations much as Valentine does at the foot of p. 57.

104 Your tea ... – Valentine's point parallels Thomasina's about rice pudding (p. 6) and they use the same word, 'odd'.

105 'I had a dream ...' – the opening lines of Byron's poem 'Darkness' (1816).

106 hare's breadth – Stoppard convicts Byron not only of apparently cheating the twelve-year-old Augustus out of his kill, but also of this pun.

– *joke* – the joke Augustus does not get is that 'free will' is incompatible with being 'determined' (see this book pp. 174–5).

107 Let them ... calculus – see p. 80.

108 A prize essay – Paris was the centre of such studies: in 1807 Jean-Baptiste Fourier had written about heat flow. The French scientist most relevant is Sadi Carnot, founder of thermodynamics; but he was only sixteen in 1812. The essay is about the passing of heat from one body to another, which is why Septimus can humorously agree that it is 'about' the 'waltz'.

- the atoms do not go ... – Newton believed that every process in time could be reversed, but the problems experienced with early steam engines (see Thomasina's summaries on pp. 116–7) showed that this was untrue.
- Paris is the capital ... – Septimus seizes the opportunity, rare these days, to make his pupil seem silly.

110 such a disturbance – a tease for the audience, since they (though not Lady Croom) have been disturbed by Chloe's shout from nearly two centuries later. But the steam pump represents the Industrial Revolution, a fundamental disturbance of society.
- sulk – because he is jealous of Lady Croom's attentions to Count Zelinsky.
- not manners – because of Thomasina's failure to reply.

111 I approve of geometry – what is in fact going on is a class in drawing, not geometry; and in any case the geometry Lady Croom 'approves of' is exactly the classical regularity which was already making her daughter impatient three years ago (p. 49). But her words are also a provisional peace-offering to her former lover Septimus, whose reply is superbly ambiguous. Lady Croom's 'do not despair of it' is less so; she probably enjoys keeping both Septimus and Zelinsky in tow.
- 'Culpability' – blameworthiness – in contrast to 'Capability' Brown (see p. 37) whose designs Noakes is busy destroying.
- For the widow's ... – Lady Croom's speech reveals that the two Chaters referred to on p. 29 were one and the same, and Hannah simultaneously finds in a garden book the same information – which proves

Bernard's whole story about Byron false.

Chatsworth – Derbyshire home of the Duke of Devonshire, at whose London house Lady Croom saw Byron ('lording' is a small pun).

leaves the road at every corner – because the paper about heat flow shows a weakness in Newton's physics, the absolute determinism outlined on p. 7 ('the formula for all the future') is discredited. Thomasina is of course trying to plot the 'corners' or curves which ordinary geometry ignores.

– this gentleman – writer of the Paris essay.

– The action of bodies in heat – is Thomasina consciously teasing her mother with the double meaning here? Stoppard is certainly teasing his audience.

112 The Chater – works brilliantly in two quite different ways. If it refers to the flowers which Thomasina is touching, named after their discoverer, then she is thinking of their unpredictable detail, their 'chaos; but 'in a weekend' rather more suggests the chaos caused in a country house by those such as Mrs Chater (described by Lady Croom as 'the Chater' on p. 94).

– Hobbes – Thomas Hobbes (1588–1679) published *Leviathan* in 1651: it takes a generally low view of humanity.

– pyramids ... cones – the two shapes she has been set to draw.

– Euclid – fourth-century BC Greek mathematician, who laid down the classical geometry Thomasina has studied. The next sentence tells us she has not forgotten her thirteen-year-old's dream of discovering 'another geometry'; and also sets up

Septimus's next line: her repeated 'error' may have been a 'trial' to him.

– eligibility – suitability for marriage; i.e., girls should not know too much.

113 ... your mother and Count Zelinsky – no mention of Lord Croom. Though critical of Lady Caroline Lamb, Lady Croom seems to have paraded herself in the company of two male escorts, her young former lover and (we surmise) her present one.

being sketched ... – this destroys Bernard on p. 83.

– for a Lamb – Byron was sketched with Lady Caroline Lamb, and the proverbial expression is 'as well be hanged for a sheep as for a lamb'.

– bull in a china shop – traditional for someone who smashes up everything.

114 Newcomen – Thomas Newcomen produced his first steam pump a century earlier, in 1712; it was extremely inefficient and a series of improvements were developed later.

– cottage – see p. 127.

115 ... room for a piano? – Septimus wants to banish Count Zelinsky and his waltzes to the hermitage – but that is where he himself will end up.

from Paris! – the paper shows that any heat engine will give back less than was put into it (a 'shilling' was twelve 'pence').

116 this business – of Thomasina's education. In 1812 a young girl should not be ahead of her tutor; it is time to marry her off.

– *Ce soir* ... – please speak French this evening.

– know it about engines – 'they' have not understood the wider significance, which is that the reversibility inherent in Newtonian physics is false. There is an 'arrow of time' travelling only one way.

117 being a Septimus – the name means 'seventh child'. We incidentally learn how at so early an age Septimus came to be reviewing Chater's poetry for a London publication.

118 You must not ... – Septimus's response to fifteen-year-old Augustus is a model of quick tact and kindness. 'I must rely ... ignorance' boosts the boy's self-esteem, though he will soon discover that actually Thomasina is correctly informed (by Septimus himself three years earlier).

120 as sure as he shot that hare – but (see p. 106) he probably didn't.

121 Except Hannah./I'll come and watch – why? Hannah does eventually dress up (next page), but not for the photograph, and as inconspicuously as possible. Has she refused point-blank to appear in the photograph? or has Chloe automatically excluded her? Either way, Hannah is kept separate from a prevailing playfulness.

– Bo-Peep – nursery-rhyme shepherdess: perhaps the elder brother's view of Chloe, whereas she sees herself as the mature witty observer Jane Austen (1775–1817). Valentine's 'Of course' may, however, see Austen as a cliché choice.

122 Oh! – all she is after (or at least would admit she is after) is a lesson in waltzing.

123 Mr Hodge! – a sudden mock-formality, perhaps in itself flirtatious.

– Are you reading my essay? ... You have my old primer – Thomasina's rabbit equation has reminded Septimus of her grandiose marginal claim at the age

of thirteen. He senses, very uncertainly, that the
iterated equations she is now doing might actually
lead towards 'irregular geometry'. Shown the page,
Thomasina says immediately and quite lightly that
her claim was just a joke – as, in her view (see p. 8),
was Fermat's: 'a joke to make you all mad'. But
Septimus, even before her death, is becoming
hooked.

124 If mama comes – as with the kiss on the previous
page, Thomasina seems naively confident in the
sexual innocence of what she is doing; and yet
subconsciously she is seducing Septimus. On p. 129
she does admit it, to herself and to him.

127 that cottage – the hermitage (see p. 114), in which
Septimus first kissed Thomasina; and which was
Noakes's replacement for the previous gazebo, in
which Septimus and Byron were seen conducting
amours. The parallelism is extended as the
theodolite recalls Noakes's spy-glass.

– Of course not. What for? – eighteen-year-old Chloe
has tried to seem casual and hardened about sex;
but here leaps for the romantic solution, running
away with Bernard. He is the one truly casual and
hardened.

128 A scrape – Bernard is quoting Hannah back at
herself: see p. 42, where he resisted the word as too
mild. Of course no one today is going to challenge
him to a duel.

129 in blind faith – because it is beyond his own
understanding.

– Be careful with the flame – this and the play's
remaining moments are discussed above, this book,
pp. 199–200.

Criticisms

These plays have not pleased everyone. The present book is written by an enthusiast and its aim is to assist with study rather than provide a full spread of critical opinion. But this chapter will discuss various reservations which have been expressed about Stoppard's achievement. Some of them he might also have voiced himself: he is engagingly modest and realistic about his craft and the difficulties it gives him.

Withdrawing with Style from the Chaos

The phrase comes from Lord Malquist in Stoppard's novel (see this book, p. 17) and was used as the title of Kenneth Tynan's highly readable profile of Stoppard in his 1979 book *Show People*. Tynan was a very powerful theatre critic who also helped to set up the National Theatre; he knew Stoppard quite well and presents some vivid anecdotes: Tom as agile wicketkeeper and batsman winning a match for Harold Pinter's cricket team, Tom talking of lunching with the Queen at Buckingham Palace, Tom at an Oxford college quoting Bertrand Russell word-for-word to A. J. Ayer, and this 'after five hours of steady alcoholic intake'. Though the profile is ostensibly affectionate and admiring, it becomes unmistakeably a put-down, trying to equate its subject with his own cynical Malquist, as opposed to Moon. A contrast is set up between Stoppard and his contemporary and fellow-

Czech Vaclav Havel, the comic and politically dissident dramatist whom Stoppard also supported and who became – though long after Tynan's death – the first president of a Czechoslovakia freed from Communism. (It remains altogether impossible to imagine a Britain ruled by Tom Stoppard, though the fantasy has its attractions.) Tynan presents Havel as heroic and Tom as a smoothie who steers away from commitment; he even quotes one of Stoppard's supposed 'friends' as saying, 'I don't think there's anything he'd go to the guillotine for.' Much of this, especially Havel's heroism, Stoppard might in fact accept. But he certainly feels Tynan's profile was harsh, and he has taken the trouble to challenge it on one particular detail – Tynan's claim that he himself made large helpful cuts in *Jumpers* at the rehearsal stage; this Stoppard absolutely denies.

What Tynan's profile represents is the left-wing orthodoxy of many theatre people, who claim that the higher purpose of their craft is to raise political awareness. As it happens, and as Tynan admits, some of Stoppard's own best work has also been aimed at raising political awareness – of violations of human rights. But he was targeting Communist governments rather than those of the West, and that, in theatre circles, was less politically correct.

Clearly expecting his reader to disapprove, Tynan twice quotes an article by Stoppard in which he defends 'Western liberal democracy favouring an intellectual elite and a progressive middle class'. That doesn't seem unreasonable today; and in any case it is a position altogether different from that of the appalling Malquist, who declares, 'Style, dear boy, style. There is nothing else.' Moon (and we may remember Stoppard's saying,

'I'm a Moon myself') is shocked by this; in his head, and in italics, he insists, *There is everything else.*

Tynan is sniping more at Stoppard's life than at his work. But certainly the profile reminds us, if we needed it, of the social limitations of the plays. Stoppard himself has occasionally admitted that all his characters tend to talk like him; the plays' range of reference is generally that of a middle-class, educated and probably south-British audience – they are, amongst other things, clever pieces for the chattering classes, smart events to be seen at. This inevitably antagonises some people (as does over-praise, such as that of the columnist Bernard Levin, who rashly compared Stoppard to no less a figure than Mozart). Beckett's *Waiting for Godot* is said to succeed in prisons; *Rosencrantz* might have a stickier time, because it depends so much on cultural knowledge and clever talk. Stoppard knows this well enough, and has always been clear about where he is coming from.

Episodic Rather Than Organic

> I tend to write through a series of small, large and microscopic ambushes ... My preoccupation ... takes the form of contriving to inject some sort of interest and colour into every line, rather than counting on the general situation having a general interest which will hold an audience ... *Jumpers* ... breaks its neck to be entertaining.

This was spoken at the time of *Travesties* (to the editors of *Theatre Quarterly*), and is a characteristically honest account of the first three plays studied in this book. What is significantly missing is any mention of *development*. An audience is happy enough to be entertained moment by moment; but after an old-style variety show it could emerge outside on the pavement retaining nothing more than a consciousness of time pleasantly passed. The charge against Stoppard is a bit like the cliché complaint about Chinese food, that it doesn't satisfy; an hour later you're hungry again. The plays glitter, but they don't actually illuminate; in another adapted cliché, the whole may be less than the sum of its parts.

Such strictures seem to me at least partially fair: Stoppard's plays are generally better at moments than at development. This is partly structural but partly also moral and philosophical: the 'A but minus A' formula demands that one persuasive utterance is followed by another which is also as persuasive as possible. But this makes it difficult to reach an ending, let alone a natural *outcome*. Stoppard tends to finish his plays with a final excellent theatrical *moment*, rather than with a true resolution.

But that, to be fair, is a common tendency in late-twentieth-century drama: it has been an age with some distaste for resolutions. And I am sure that Stoppard's writing in the almost twenty years between *Travesties* and *Arcadia* has deepened and developed – in practice in traditional directions: towards cumulative plots which gather the spectator emotionally, and towards some elements of psychological realism. With *Arcadia* itself, Stoppard won over many of his doubters, while to old fans like me it was what we had always been waiting for – in 1982 I wrote of my dream that Stoppard would some day write 'like a modern Chekhov', and here he comes quite near to it. Written within its writer's middle-aged, conservative decorum, *Arcadia* maintains all that was best in the young Stoppard: theatrical surprise, word-play and a genuine concern for fundamental questions about existence and morality; it is incidentally more up-to-date, in the maths and the theories, than his earlier plays; and it has also a strong story-line (the element which Stoppard says he finds hardest). Because it is more realist than most of his earlier work it can grow 'organically', rather than as a jumble of scenes. *Arcadia* has no need to begin with any sort of circus stunt; its first line – a thirteen-year-old asking about sex – is enough to grip an audience instantly, and leads towards a central idea: that people fall in love according to 'chaos' rather than Newton, unpredictably and apparently randomly. The play then proceeds with something of the structure of a detective story (though we are worlds away from *The Real Inspector Hound*) and it generates intense cumulative curiosity and anxiety: its many laughs seem to come *incidental* to its story, as do the laughs in real life.

He Can't Do Women

This charge, often made in the 1970s, never convinced me: I reckon Tom Stoppard can 'do', with theatrical competence, most things he chooses to. But when the criticism is re-phrased as 'he marginalises women' it becomes more damaging. Attitudes in early Stoppard are entirely those of the British, dominant, single-sex-educated male. In *Rosencrantz*, not only are there no female characters (outside Shakespeare) but they aren't even missed. Any hint of sex is merely adolescent: Ros's grubby curiosity and Guil's alarmed recoiling. They lament their uncertainty and isolation, but without reference to the absence of love, or even of female company. To be fair, part of the point of the play is that they don't have lives outside it, and there is one finely Freudian moment on p. 29, when Guil speaks of forgetting how to spell words and chooses as examples 'wife' and 'house', that indicates a dramatist aware of what he's doing. But where women do appear in Stoppard's early plays they tend to be seen through what feminists call 'the male gaze'. Both women in *Jumpers* are seen naked, the Secretary in a striptease, Dotty as a stage star; the Secretary, though onstage virtually throughout, isn't given a single word to speak, let alone a name; and Dotty equally stereotypically represents exasperating, yet of course lovable, feminine irrationality. Cecily in *Travesties* is required, in a quite un-Wildean way, to perform an erotic dance, and Gwendolen to read aloud to Tzara a suggestive re-organisation of a Shakespeare sonnet; both are cast as personal assistants to male maestros, Lenin and Joyce; while Wilde's intimidating Lady Bracknell is, perhaps significantly, relocated in a male character, James Joyce. These are women admitted only in subservience, or as decoration, to inter-male discourses about reality, morality, art and political power.

But in 1978 *Night and Day* was a conscious answer to such charges: a psychologically realist play with a woman as the central character and the audience allowed access to her thoughts and fantasies as well as to her speech. Two later plays, *Hapgood* and *Indian Ink*, are also built around central female roles. And in *Arcadia*, though sex is constantly in the air, we have progressed far beyond the male-gazing cartoons of a quarter of a century earlier: Hannah (as the only one not in love) is a shrewd anchor-figure, and Thomasina is a marvellous – and respectful – study of female adolescence. It is important to recognise that three of the four plays studied in this book come from the early years of a long career; and although I enjoy them and other youthful work such as *The Real Inspector Hound, After Magritte* and the superb radio play *Artist Descending a Staircase*, Stoppard's later achievement does seem to me more considerable.

All Head and No Heart

This is perhaps the commonest charge against Tom Stoppard, particularly from those who have only seen one or two early plays; again it seems less relevant to the later work. Michael Billington (*In Conversation: Billington*) produces an interesting alternative argument. He suggests – admittedly partly because he is writing about the spy-play *Hapgood* – that Stoppard has an emotional 'double identity'; and that this is crucial to the plays as well. They 'have been analysed as if they were intellectual conceits. I suspect they only work because of their emotional ground-base.' He also quotes Stoppard himself saying:

> I am a very emotional person. People wish to perceive me as someone who works out ideas in a cool, dis-passionate way but I don't think that's my personality at all.

Some people's inner sense of themselves may cause them to compensate in public, trying to behave in the opposite way. Friends of Stoppard have often spoken of his air of security, of being at ease with the world. He is certainly aware of his good fortune, not only in his adult prosperity but in being in England at all, in a stable, liberal democracy. The facts of his earliest years are that he was twice a refugee, losing his father (whom he does not remember), that he was at boarding-schools between

235

the ages of seven and seventeen, that English was the second language he learned – and that in India – and that he came to this country only at the age of nine. Even his description of intense childhood happiness, one moment of white light, has the effect of casting darkness elsewhere; the words come from a radio play, *Where Are They Now?*, but are almost identical with those in an autobiographical article ('Going Back', *Independent* Sat/Sun Magazine, 23 March 1991):

> I remember once – I was seven, my first term at prep school – I remember walking down one of the corridors, trailing my finger along a raised edge along the wall, and I was suddenly totally happy ... everywhere I looked, in my mind, *nothing was wrong.*

This is offered as a precious memory; but its extreme poignancy lies in its glimpse of a seven-year-old only too accustomed to checking around ('everywhere I looked') and to finding things that *were* wrong. My impression is that the young Stoppard, like the seven-year-old, looked very warily about him, with emotional security as a high priority; and that the appearance of being at ease with the world, and the cartoon manner of his early plays, are highly self-protective rather than indifferent. His plays are frequently about psychological pain, even when the characters are exaggerated to the point where we have to laugh at them: in the plays studied in this book, the outstanding examples are Dotty and George. Acute pain and emotion are *implied* in later plays such as *Every Good Boy Deserves Favour* (1977), the more vividly for being understated; or indeed at times in *Arcadia* – the letter that Septimus writes to Lady Croom to be read in the event of his death (*Arcadia*, p. 91) or the final exchanges between

Septimus and Thomasina. Stoppard is unlikely to write plays in which characters sob their hearts out or go for each other with kitchen knives (the nearest is perhaps *The Real Thing*, 1982); but that doesn't at all mean that his work is all head and no heart. As long ago as 1982, when first writing about him, I called my final chapter 'Caring', because that seemed to me such a strong element in his work. Where Tynan emphasised the Malquist, I find far more of Mr Moon.

Charm

The more damaging accusation may in fact be not that Stoppard's work is cold-blooded but roughly the opposite: that it is inclined to be soft-centred. John Simon in the *Hudson Review* (1967) called the idea of *Rosencrantz* 'a conception of genius, which requires genius to develop it; whereas, in the event, it gets only cleverness and charm'. Robert Brustein (*The Third Theatre*, 1970) found it 'a noble conception' spoilt by 'a prevailing strain of cuteness ... As an artist, Stoppard does not fight hard enough for his insights'; and – still on *Rosencrantz*, in *Encounter* in July 1967 – John Weightman commented on Guil's 'tongueless dwarf' speech:

> The bird out of season and the tongueless dwarf are surely *kitsch*, but are we meant to appreciate them as being symptomatic of Guildenstern's camp vibration, or to enjoy them as poetry? I suspect Mr Stoppard is hoping for the latter reaction but would settle for the former.

I think this last is well argued. Making things 'work' in the theatre – about which Stoppard often speaks – does involve 'settling' for compromises, but that should not mean that anything goes. He is frank about seeing theatre as a 'recreation', about aiming to entertain; and his wish to have his plays *liked* is itself likeable, as well as good for the box-office; but for more than thirty years spectators have felt him to be an artist capable of more than mere box-office success. This is perhaps the most crucial 'A, yet minus A' of all. In one of Stoppard's best self-diagnoses, to Ronald Hayman in 1976, he imagined 'sirens on a rock saying, "Come on, come away from the serious artists." I never quite know whether I want to be a serious artist or a siren.' (The sirens, in Greek myth, charmed sailors to their destruction.)

My own view is that we ourselves have to 'settle' for this ambivalence in Stoppard, and then celebrate it. Although he has shown more open seriousness in later years, and the plays have become less flashy, he is not a Prince Hamlet of literature, nor was meant to be. He once said that watching Beckett or Pinter made him feel as if he'd been made in Hong Kong (i.e., cheap imitation goods); this was over-modest, but an accurate perception that he is not that *kind* of 'serious artist'. The mixture of junk and James Joyce is not only distinctive to Stoppard, it is also what he's best at, and where he is actually original. It can make his work disappointing to the highest expectations (Simon and Brustein, above, using words such as 'genius' and 'noble', seemed to be setting *Rosencrantz* against the greatest comic writers such as Shakespeare or Chekhov) but it can also make it exciting, and occasionally revelatory. Above all, in *Arcadia* Stoppard's ability to charm is integrated within an intricate and poignant structure, which leaves no feeling of awkward compromise but is entirely satisfying.

Select Bibliography

Other Works of Tom Stoppard
For the interplay between dandy and would-be-good:
Stoppard's one novel, *Lord Malquist and Mr Moon*,
London: Faber and Faber, 1966.

For the bizarre explaining itself:
After Magritte, in *Stoppard: Plays One*, London: Faber
and Faber, 1993.

For *Jumpers*:
Another Moon Called Earth, in *Stoppard: Plays Three*,
London: Faber and Faber, 1998.

For *Travesties*:
Artist Descending a Staircase, in *Tom Stoppard: Plays
Two*, London: Faber and Faber, 1996.

Interviews with Tom Stoppard
The following are helpful collections:

Paul Delaney (ed.), *Tom Stoppard In Conversation*,
    Michigan: University of Michigan Press, 1994.
Mel Gussow, *Conversations with Stoppard*, London:
    Nick Hern Books, 1995; New York: Grove/Atlantic,
    Inc.
Ronald Hayman, *Tom Stoppard*, London: Heinemann,
    1979.

Critical Studies

A small selection which offers useful guidance. If out of print, copies may be found in libraries.

Tim Brassell, *Tom Stoppard: An Assessment*, London: Macmillan, 1985.

John Harty III (ed.), *Tom Stoppard, A Casebook*, Garland Inc., 1988.

Ronald Hayman, *Tom Stoppard*, London: Heinemann, 1979.

Jim Hunter: *Tom Stoppard's Plays*, London: Faber and Faber, 1982.

Anthony Jenkins: *The Theatre of Tom Stoppard*, Cambridge: Cambridge University Press, 1990.

Roger Sales: *Rosencrantz and Guildenstern Are Dead*, London: Penguin, 1988.